Food Fights

First published in 1993, this title explores the underlying ideologies and decision-making procedures that codify the rules of the post-World War II liberal, now defunct Soviet socialist, mercantilist and South preferential trade regimes. *Food Fights* presents a rich case study and rigorous data analysis of organised agricultural trade that uncovers similarities between these diverse economic systems and identifies the principle trends governing the new global economy.

Food Fights

International Regimes and the Politics of
Agricultural Trade Disputes

Renée Marlin-Bennett

Routledge
Taylor & Francis Group

First published in 1993
by Gordon and Breach

This edition first published in 2010 by Routledge
2 Park Square, Milton Park, Abingdon, Oxon, OX14 4RN

Simultaneously published in the USA and Canada
by Routledge
270 Madison Avenue, New York, NY 10016

Routledge is an imprint of the Taylor & Francis Group, an informa business

Publisher's Note

The publisher has gone to great lengths to ensure the quality of this reprint but points
out that some imperfections in the original copies may be apparent.

Disclaimer

The publisher has made every effort to trace copyright holders and welcomes
correspondence from those they have been unable to contact.

ISBN 13: 978-0-415-56713-8 (hbk)
ISBN 13: 978-0-203-85985-8 (ebk)

ISBN 10: 0-415-56713-0 (hbk)
ISBN 10: 0-203-85985-5 (ebk)

FOOD FIGHTS

FOOD FIGHTS

International Regimes and the Politics of Agricultural Trade Disputes

Renée Marlin-Bennett

School of International Service
The American University
Washington, DC

Gordon and Breach
USA • Switzerland • Australia • Belgium • France
Germany • Great Britain • India • Japan • Malaysia
Netherlands • Russia • Singapore

Gordon and Breach Science Publishers

820 Town Center Drive
Langhorne, Pennsylvania 19047
United States of America

Glinkastrasse 13 = 15
O-1086 Berlin
Germany

Y-Parc
Chemin de la Sallaz
1400 Yverdon, Switzerland

Post Office Box 90
Reading, Berkshire RG1 8JL
Great Britain

Private Bag 8
Camberwell, Victoria 3124
Australia

3-14-9, Okubo
Shinjuku-ku, Tokyo 169
Japan

58, rue Lhomond
75005 Paris
France

Emmaplein 5
1075 AW Amsterdam
Netherlands

Library of Congress Cataloging-in-Publication Data

Marlin-Bennett, Renée, 1959–
    Food fights : international regimes and the politics of
agricultural trade disputes / Renée Marlin-Bennett.
        p.   cm.
    Includes bibliographical references (p.   ).
    ISBN 2-88124-588-9
    1. Tariff on farm produce. 2. Produce trade—Government policy.
3. Agriculture and state. 4. Free trade. 5. Protectionism.
6. International economic relations. I. Title.
    HF2651.F27A248   1993
    382'.45664—dc20   93-18535
                                                                          CIP

To the memory of my grandparents
with abiding love

CONTENTS

FIGURES

TABLES

ACKNOWLEDGEMENTS

I am extremely grateful to the many students, colleagues and senior scholars, friends, and family members who have supported my efforts to write this book, who have offered constructive criticism, and who have put up with me when I was in the grips of writer's *crise*. Of the students, Elizabeth Arias and Kimberly Holloman Alexander deserve special mention. The late Edward E. Azar of the University of Maryland gave me both academic guidance when he served as an outside reader on my dissertation committee and material support when he gave me an office and an intellectual community at the Center for International Development and Conflict Management. My two dissertation committee members from MIT, Lincoln P. Bloomfield and the chairman, Hayward R. Alker, Jr., pointed the way toward major improvements in my work. Professor Alker has continued providing guidance on this research in the years since the completion of my doctorate, and I believe that my theoretical contribution to international relations is most consonant with his scholarship.

At the American University, School of International Service Dean Louis W. Goodman and Department of International Politics and Foreign Policy Chair Philip Brenner have provided comments and encouragement. If my writing is intelligible, it is because of the admonitions of Professor John Richardson. Professor Nicholas G. Onuf tirelessly read through draft after draft of each chapter, helping me to clarify propositions and hone arguments. His scholarship on the role of rules in international relations has been particularly influential. Without his constant prodding, I do not think I would have finished this work.

The greatest share of gratitude goes to my wonderful family. My husband, who now has the distinction of being the astronomer most knowledgeable about theories of international regimes, has always been there to help in every way possible. Our parents have always encouraged me, and our son has been a source of delightful distraction when distraction was needed.

Chapter 1

Introduction

In a world where the US-Soviet rivalry has left center stage, attention now focuses on international economic competition. Nations are becoming increasingly interdependent, and disputes over international trade policies are now among the most serious of international conflicts. What was once "low politics" has become the stuff of "high politics." Trade has been promoted. The gravity of trade disputes in today's world should not be underestimated. The conditions triggering trade disputes and the trade disputes themselves can have serious deleterious effects. The availability of goods and unstable prices can affect the livelihood and well-being of virtually everyone. No society is untouched.

Food and feed are two categories of commodities for which the relationship between trade disputes and people's lives is particularly compelling. Food for humans and feed for livestock are vital for survival. People of the developing world, as well as the industrialized world, are vulnerable to changes in supply and access to foreign markets. When trade disputes disrupt markets and when states' policies conflict, people suffer. And, according to United Nations Food and Agriculture Organization Director General Edouard Saouma, the harm from agricultural trade problems falls disproportionately on the less prosperous countries.

> Agriculture is the most important economic base for most developing countries, which also depend heavily on exports of agriculture, fishery and forestry products to earn much-needed foreign exchange. Unfortunately, the situation concerning trade in these products is very disquieting. Problems affecting trade in agriculture, fishery and forestry products have persisted since the early 1980s. And, in some respects, such as export prices and market access, the situation has worsened.[1]

Yet at the same time, changes in agricultural production have led to deleterious effects on the farming sectors of industrialized countries. As an American official explained, United States agriculture has had relentless growth in productivity. Consumption is increasing at a lower rate. The consequence is that the US will either need to export more or shrink agriculture, and the same is true for

1

Canada, the European Community, Australia, and other developed exporters.[2]

The pressure to export agricultural goods on the part of both developing and industrialized countries sets the stage for problems to occur. The frequency of food and feed trade disputes and their effects challenge students of international relations to understand the political, economic, and social context in which this form of international conflict occurs. The human implications of agricultural trade disputes and the inability of previous theoretical works, especially in the field of international political economy, to deal with agricultural trade motivates this work. How and why do trade disputes transpire? Traditional studies of conflict do not provide the answer because classical notions of power, predicated on the use of physical force, do not apply.

The area of political science that customarily studies the politics of trade is international political economy. Scholars in this field are currently more concerned with explaining unexpected cooperation, rather than conflict. They propose theories of international regimes —sets of principles, norms, and rules which guide the behavior of states—to explain cooperation (Keohane and Nye, 1977; Krasner, 1982; Ruggie, 1982). Consequently, regimes theorists have not looked at how regimes might affect conflict. Moreover, they have often looked at agriculture as an exception to regime ordered trade.

This study offers a revised theory of regimes that can explain conflict processes. I support the theory by analyzing cases of food and feed trade problems. The use of food and feed trade problems for the case studies reflects the significance of food and feed trade to all those who earn their living in agriculture and to all those for whom food is less than plentiful, from the mildly malnourished to the starving. In the industrialized democracies, the importance of food and feed trade disputes can be seen in the increased politicking on the issue. Farm lobbies and consumer groups press for changes in public policy. Governments try to effect change through negotiations with other countries over agriculture. For example, representatives of the United States and Japan have negotiated the elimination of Japanese barriers to beef and citrus imports.

Welfare issues become even more apparent in the case of developing countries (and some East European countries). Some have argued that the world produces enough food to nourish all people adequately and that the malnourished suffer from problems of global distribution. Trade disputes hinder the distribution of food.

The problem is not only the supply of foodstuffs to areas plagued by hunger; it is also the inability of impoverished farmers to earn needed cash when international markets are closed to them. Agriculture is one sector that is often strictly protected by industrialized countries. A 1988 World Bank report estimated that developing countries lost between 2.5 and 9 percent of their GNP due to the protectionism of industrialized countries (*World Development Report*, 1988, p. 16). An earlier study asserted that barrier free trade in beef and sugar would increase foreign export earnings of developing countries by between $6.6 billion and more than $12 billion (Zietz and Valdés, 1986).[3] According to the United Nations' *1987 International Trade Statistics Yearbook* data for 1986, the developing market economy countries exported 29.4 percent of the food, live animals, beverages, and tobacco traded in the world. They imported 20.1 percent. For developing market economy countries in America and Oceania, agricultural exports composed 34.4 and 41.1 percent, respectively, of their total exports. These statistics reveal the vulnerability of the poorer countries to obstacles to agricultural trade. Impeding the flow of agricultural goods severely affects them.

WHY SHOULD PEOPLE WHO CARE ABOUT TRADE CARE ABOUT THEORY?

Theorists of international relations are predisposed, from the outset, to care about theoretical issues. For many of us, the debate over regimes theory and the different variants of regimes theory, logical consistency, and empirical validity provide sufficient fodder for substantial interest in a work. But this book is a theoretical treatment of the politics of *agricultural trade*, and trade is inherently practical and substantive. Theorize as we might about trade, it goes on, day after day. Business people, government officials, and farmers who know nothing (and care less) about theories of international relations meet and arrange to buy and sell food and feed all the time. Why, then, should theory matter at all?

If all trade went completely smoothly, then I would argue that a rudimentary knowledge of comparative advantage and a good deal of common business sense would be all the theory that anyone would need to be good at trading or at analyzing trade. But trade does not go smoothly: Witness the 1992 revival of the old US-EC oilseeds trade dispute that threatened to derail global progress on the Uruguay Round of the Multilateral Trade Negotiations.

Theory allows generalization and categorization; it explains, predicts, and shows trends. The theory that I develop here points to otherwise hidden explanations and predictions of trade conflict and, more specifically, of agricultural trade conflict. Often, news stories about trade problems focus on the details: We want Japan to import x more tons of oranges and y more tons of lemons. Instead, the theory that I present here leads to questions about the rules that underlie the discrete protest, for it is these rules—be they adhered to or violated, just or unjust—that recur as the sources of conflict over trade. While the specific items and quantities traded are unique to a particular dispute, the rules at stake come up over and over again as the fundamental cause of many disputes. Theorizing about why cases of trade disputes are similar or different can help avoid or ameliorate conflict and facilitate trade. The theory that is presented here points to the way in which certain rules under certain circumstances become contentious.

The theory presented here is relevant for people interested in the general subject of trade and in the more specific area of agricultural trade. Trade generalists will gain insight into:

- the sources of trade problems and disputes from differing beliefs about how trade ought to be conducted;

- the conditions that are most likely to precipitate the outbreak of a trade dispute;

- the Catch 22 of preferential agreements such as the Sugar Protocol of the Lomé Convention;

- the ease with which commodity agreements can be coopted to preserve the market dominance of strong trading states;

- the circumvention of the liberal nature of the GATT by some trade policies; and

- the trend toward a more mercantile organization of trade in the wake of the end of the Soviet bloc, despite the privatization of Eastern Europe.

Readers with a special interest in food trade will find new views of

- the way agricultural trade, contrary to the common wisdom, *is* organized according to internationally (but not universally) accepted rules;

- the tension, particularly acute in agricultural trade, between rules that make economic sense and rules that make political and social sense; and,

- through the case study (Chapter 4), the complexity of sugar trade.

I hope that a governmental policy analyst who has read this work and who is charged with examining the wisdom of recommending that the US sign a new sugar agreement (let's say) will look not just to the numbers (who gets what quota; how much is the US required to import) and not just to the specific rules of the agreement (buffer stocks? dispute conciliation procedures?), but also to the claims made by the participants. Is this agreement's purpose to stabilize prices? To provide for the redistribution of market shares in favor of developing countries? To preserve the sovereign right of states to protect their domestic industries? Moreover, how does this agreement conflict with or complement existing trade rules of the GATT? Could policies allowed or even advocated by the GATT be disallowed by this new agreement? What kinds of disputes are likely to occur because of incompatible rules? By suggesting to the analyst what important questions to ask, theory becomes usable.

A VARIATION ON REGIME THEORY

The theory that I have applied to this study is a variation of regime theory. First, what is regime theory as it is normally conceived? Theorists of international regimes suggest that policy makers have conflicting interests. If each acts atomistically, the gains of one will result in the losses of another. However, policy makers from different countries could *rationally* cooperate if they were reasonably certain that their trading partners would follow the same rules that they had committed to uphold. Greater certainty about each other's behavior could then result in more beneficial outcomes for all and a mutual interest in maintaining the cooperative system. A key assumption of these theorists is that conflict is a conflict of interests. Creating certainty about further cooperation by developing an international regime circumvents the conflict of interests by providing a set of rules. Trade that is organized by regime rules should, on the face of it, end the conflicts.

Yet agriculture has been seen as the exception to regimes theory. The General Agreement on Tariffs and Trade (GATT) has been notoriously bad at regulating trade in agriculture (Schuh, 1986).[4] The United States, for example, has a waiver that exempts it from applying GATT rules to certain agricultural imports. Since the US is a major exporter and importer of agricultural goods, its abrogation of GATT responsibilities weakens the control of the GATT for agriculture.

Either there is something unique about agriculture that prevents cooperation from evolving and ameliorating trade disputes, or regimes theory needs some fine-tuning to account for conflict. In this book, I argue the latter. Regarding agricultural trade as ungoverned by rules misses both the amount of discussion about agriculture at the GATT and the alternative rules for agricultural trade developed under different auspices. A revised version of regimes theory, one that accounts for how people create and choose rules, identifies contending sets of agricultural trade rules and helps explain the conditions of both trade conflict and cooperation in this sector. By doing so, I pursue three goals: to increase our understanding of trade disputes as a form of international conflict, to show the pervasive influence of international regimes on policy makers' behavior, and to identify the political and ideological roots of trade regimes.

Regimes theorists have not examined how regimes cause conflict for two reasons. First, regimes theory was developed to explain cooperation. In the realist and neo-realist conceptions, the theoretical progenitors of regimes theory, conflict is understood to be a natural condition of international relations. Since conflict is natural, and not a variable to be explained, it is simply not the subject of regimes theory. I do not accept this premise. Moreover, I will show that regimes theory, when amended, explains conflict as well as cooperation, thereby making it a richer explanatory theory.

The second reason is more pernicious because it is unconscious: There is a dominant Western bias in the writings on the subject. This bias, in turn, leads to two questionable assumptions: that each state wishes to maximize its wealth and that the participants have come to a consensus about what issues the regime will regulate. The assumption that each party wishes to maximize its wealth presupposes a neo-liberal understanding of the State as a Rational Actor. I reject the analytical fiction that a state can be viewed as a unitary, rational actor. States are complex organizations of human beings. Even though all states have the same function—providing governance for their citizens—it is too simplistic to conclude that all states have the same utility function. The human beings who comprise governments have different preferences. Policy makers need not share a Western preference to maximize wealth. People have different beliefs about what is good, right, and just. Therefore people's preferences differ. By examining the relationship between ideology and the trade rules that policy makers advocate, I begin to show where trade policy preferences come from and how they have explanatory and predictive power. The rules that people develop for trade will reflect the beliefs and preferences of policy makers.

Similarly, different cultures will draw different boundaries around an issue area. The most commonly used definition of regime is Krasner's: "a set of principles, norms, rules, and decision-making procedures around which the expectations of actors converge for a given area in international relations" (1982). To look for regimes, scholars have grounded their research in specific focused case studies. Given this methodology, the authors have examined very sharply circumscribed sets of relations. Some have looked at trade, implicitly among GATT members; others have looked at trade in commodities. The result of the narrow focus is that they tend to assume a liberal international political economy, often with a social welfare complexion. (See, for example, E. Haas, 1980; Lipson, 1982; Ruggie, 1982; and Finlayson and Zacher, 1988. Young and Aggarwal are exceptions.) These authors assume that deviations from accepted practices are weaknesses in the regime or comprise some evolutionary or devolutionary process. (See E. Haas, 1983.)

This is a useful definition only when we wish to look at very narrowly defined issue areas, trade among industrialized market economy countries, for example. But what about trade within the Soviet bloc when it existed? Between developing countries? Between a Soviet bloc country and a Western country? Is there one operative trade regime in these cases? I think not. Instead, the participants' expectations are guided by different regimes, sometimes complementary, sometimes contradictory. When we look at global trade relations, the existence of *multiple regimes* in the area of trade, construed broadly, is more consistent with political and economic reality.

An ironic thesis emerges: International regimes, which explain how an accepted set of rules make cooperation rational, also explain conflict. Conceptions of proper trading practices and policies are articulated in regimes. Even the creation of the issue area itself— what Haggard and Simmons (1987: 497) refer to as the scope of the regime—must be a part of the regime.[5] In other words, the regime contains a rule that sets its scope. By not recognizing this rule, scholars have missed the way ideologies influence rule formation and how different ideologies generate regimes that define the scope differently. A more fruitful approach avoids confusing the scope of a regime with the regime itself.

Conflict happens when people disagree over the rules or the interpretation of the rules. This notion troubles some of the writers on international regimes. Regimes are cooperative, not conflictual, they would say. But cooperation and conflict co-exist all the time in international relations. As Keohane points out, cooperation is not harmony of interests (1984). I would emphasize that cooperation does not even necessarily indicate shared preferences among policy makers for a particular set of rules.

REDEFINING REGIMES

To explore multiple regimes and conflict in trade, regimes need to be defined to account for both their rules and their members. To alter Krasner's (1982) definition:

A regime is a set of principles, norms, rules, and decision-making procedures that create an issue area around which the perceptions and expectations of a group of actors converge.

The two changes here are that a regime creates an issue area and that a regime orders behavior for a group of actors. Focusing on the creation of the issue area and on which traders believe which rules apply better represents the practices of different groups of countries and companies. A participant-centered focus addresses the fundamental incongruity among different beliefs and practices. Focusing on participants also allows us to trace the expectations that traders have about how other traders will and ought to behave.[6]

Participants refer to alternative sets of rules that cover roughly the same issue area of food and feed trade when they make claims about who is breaking the rules for trade and how. Each of the regimes I identify in international agricultural trade provides a set of rules regularizing behaviors and orienting expectations despite the fundamental disorder of the international system. Incorporating formal treaties, international regimes can provide guidelines for orderly international trading behavior, but the inconsistencies within and among different regimes, along with gross disparities in power among the participants, result in "orderly disorder."

What have been the different regimes, judging from recent practices? Until the dissolution of the Soviet Union, political disagreements in our world were often expressed as "East versus West" or "North versus South." The compass directions provided metaphors for economic and political systems, as well as levels of development. The regions provided a sense of physical coherence to the generally consistent ideological orientations of the states. We often viewed our world as comprised of a liberal West, a Soviet East, and an emerging South. Some scholars have come to recognize a re-emergence of the mercantile North (Gilpin, 1987; Lake, 1988). The metaphor breaks down at this point because the ideological poles are not mutually exclusive; neither are the geographical regions clearly defined.[7]

Nevertheless, these political and ideological blocs provide the foundation for the formulation of trade regimes, along with the keys to predicting the future organization of trade. Until the changes in the Soviet bloc heralded by Mikhail Gorbachev's *perestroika*, there were four identifiable trade regimes:

(1) the post World War II liberal (West),

(2) the Soviet socialist (East),

(3) the mercantilist (North), and

(4) the South preferential (South).

The Soviet socialist trade regime has disappeared, but to understand the trajectory of current changes it is necessary to examine how this regime organized trade within Eastern Europe until the late 1980s.

Role of Ideology

Ideology plays an important part in generating regime rules. Identifying the ideological underpinnings of regimes demonstrates similarities of perceptions and expectations across several issue areas at different levels of specificity.[8] Postulating a single, global trade regime "nested" (Aggarwal, 1985) in a single economic regime can not account for differences between, for example, Soviet and Western trade practices from the end of World War II to 1991. It does make sense, though, to conceptualize a Soviet socialist trade regime nested in a Soviet socialist economic regime. These co-existed with a post World War II liberal trade regime nested within a post World War II liberal economic regime.

Ideologies provide the organizing principles of regimes. The term, "ideology," has come to refer to the fundamental ideas that legitimate a society, identify the Good, and define the limits of the possible.[9] Belief system, world view, *Weltanschauung*, and culture are often used the same way. Ideological thought, in these terms, is the only possible kind of thought. (This is to say that we socially construct our reality and that there is no reality outside how we perceive and conceive it.) While the constraints on each individual's thoughts are both unique and fluid, there are elements common to the thinking of most people in a society. This is the ideological core of that society.

Human beings, singly and in groups, can try to amend or replace a society's ideology. Their success will depend on how powerful they are. At the same time, ideology serves as a filter on our perceptions of the world. We are limited in what we see by the ideology of the society in which we live. We are both agents and objects of the simplifications and blinders that our society places on our understanding. This synergistic relationship between human being and his or her milieu is simply a fact of our existence.

Usually, the content of the ideological core of a society is unarticulated because it is consensual: Why talk about what everyone agrees with? In times of crisis and conflict, we articulate ideological claims as we attempt to identify the best course of action. This does not mean that ideology goes away when there is no crisis. In times of stability, ideology recedes to the background. Nevertheless, ideology still affects how we think, perhaps in a more insidious way because we are not called upon to examine it.

Different ideologies shape different regimes because ideology limits the participants and provides the definition of what is good and legitimate. What is the appropriate conduct of states? Of firms? Of individuals? What international organizations should be established; what should their duties be? The principles, norms, rules, and decision-making procedures of a trade regime are generated by the ideology underlying the regime.[10]

Four important political-economic ideologies can be conceptualized in opposed pairs: liberalism versus Marxism-Leninism, mercantilism versus social welfare-ism. The first pair represents the preference for individual versus collective decision making. The second pair represents power politics versus the pursuit of international social justice. These four ideologies have fostered the four major trade regimes. The regimes' rules differ because their underlying ideologies have different definitions of the good and the legitimate.

However, these regimes are not self-contained closed systems. Although states may be predominantly situated within one ideology and regime, individuals may hold beliefs consistent with another (Alker, 1981). The importance of the idea that these orders "interpenetrate," to use Alker's phrasing, is that some of the rules of the regimes overlap. Shared rules facilitate cooperative interaction among actors of different political and ideological stripes. If we look to which states (and other actors) are adhering to which sets of rules, we can identify separate, though overlapping, ideologically consistent regimes.

WHY INVOKE MULTIPLE REGIMES?

Most regime scholars take the one issue-one regime approach. They would argue either:

(1) that the trade regime consisted of the union of all the principles, norms, rules, and decision-making procedures for trade, regardless of their inconsistencies; or

(2) that inconsistent principles, norms, rules, and decision-making procedures indicate that trade is not ordered by an international regime.[11]

In contrast to the single regime approach, a multiple regime approach accounts for distinct sets of rules which define, regulate, and connect several issue areas. For example, a South preferential international commodity agreement which allocates market share rights and obligations orders trade very differently from a GATT-oriented set of rules which advocates freer trade or a socialist order which advocates centralized control, even though each set of rules would order trade in commodities. This analysis holds even though the commodity agreements were originally negotiated as part of the plans for an International Trade Organization. (Some commodity agreements even pre-date the ITO.) The Soviet bloc, the developing countries, and the West had very different ideas about what the rules ought to be, so regime formation went in different directions. The Soviet bloc used state to state trade, the developing countries continued to advocate a trade regime that redistributed market share rights, while the developed countries continued to advocate a GATT-centered "liberal" regime. More than one regime was generated because of the incompatible ideologies of Soviet bloc, Western, and developing countries.

In more orthodox approaches to regimes theory, these regimes might be labelled "regime contenders" since no single regime orders all international trade. Though the difference is largely semantic, I prefer to call them regimes because their distinct ideologies provide coherence, while codification of the rules provide a good measure of formality. The ideologies underlying the regimes provide the key to understanding the differences between these regimes. As Young notes,

> [R]egimes resting on socialist premises will encompass more extensive collections of rules as well as more explicit efforts to direct behavior toward the achievement of goals than *laissez faire* regimes that emphasize decentralized decision making and autonomy for individual actors. (1980:342)

In addition, regimes for specific issues are nested within regimes for more general issues (Aggarwal, 1985). I differ from Aggarwal's interpretation by emphasizing that a regime can be nested within a more general regime only if they have the same ideological base.[12] For example, the post World War II liberal trading regime certainly seems to be nested within a capitalist power-balancing (Alker, 1981) security regime that subsumes a much wider scope. In contrast, the Soviet socialist trade regime was not consistent with the capitalist power-balancing security regime since the ideological cores differed. Rather, the Soviet socialist trading regime was nested within a Soviet socialist security regime. The more issues circumscribed by the scope of a regime, the more important principles and norms are relative to specific rules. Specific rules tend to be applicable only for particularly narrow issue-areas.

The diagram below graphically depicts the differences between my definition of regimes and that of traditional regimes theorists.

Dominant Regimes and the Role of Power

Different trade regimes have existed in different historical periods. The concept of international regime implies that some sort of consensus on the rules exists across at least one border. That people in at least two states (or city-states for earlier times) agree on the rules does not mean that everybody necessarily likes them. Regimes need not be benign.[13] The analogy to domestic regimes is straightforward: A dictator may well be regarded as the legitimate head of state (domestic regime) by his or her subjects.

Hegemonic stability theory (Gilpin, 1975; Kindleberger, 1986), as adapted to regimes theory (Keohane and Nye, 1977), suggests that a

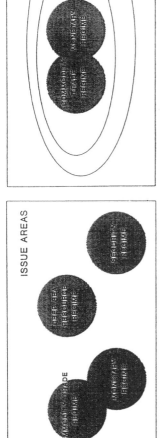

Figure 1-1.1 Usual definition

Figure 1-1.3 Young's definition

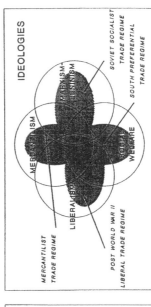

Figure 1-1.2 Aggarwal's nested regime definition

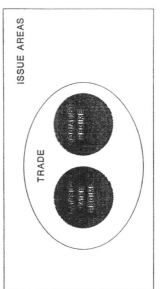

Figure 1-1.4 Multiple regime definition

Figure 1-1. Regime definitions

regime becomes dominant in a part of the world or for the entire world if it has powerful proponents. How much compliance with regime rules there is and how much of the world trades according to its rules depend on how powerful the proponents are. Classical mercantilism in the sixteenth through eighteenth centuries was dominant because of the power first of Spain and later of England, and to a lesser degree, of France. Empires are an extreme example of a very strong regime, imposed by the imperial power, that regulates both trade and political relations (Keeley, 1990). The post World War II liberal trade regime became dominant after the war because the United States made it so. The long reach of hegemonic powers allows them to enforce their preferred rules.

An alternative possibility is that a regime may become dominant because consensus is achieved through the harmonious interests or cooperative negotiations of several states (and possibly firms and international organizations). There is no theoretical reason to exclude this possibility of the development of a consensual dominant regime, and the security community of Western Europe may well fit this criterion.

More to the point is that the dominance of a particular regime does not mean that other regimes do not exist or that new regimes can not develop. The very discontent that some people feel about the imposed rules may lead them to advocate alternatives grounded in opposed ideologies. Other regimes may function outside the hegemonic reach of a dominant power (e.g., an Asian regime that coexisted with a Roman regime in ancient times; a Soviet regime that existed during the height of American dominance in the 1950s and early 1960s). Also, alternative regimes may present a challenge to the dominant state's control from within the hegemon's sphere.

As the power of the dominant state declines, the regime preferred by its policy makers may endure (Keohane, 1984). Regimes continue in place because humans, in contrast to the tendency toward entropy that governs the physical world, seek order. Regimes have staying power because they become institutionalized. The ability of policy makers to predict, with a reasonable degree of certainty, what another state or firm will do decreases the turbulence of the international system and makes decision making more efficient (Thompson, 1967).[14] At the same time, however, a decline in the power of the hegemonic state may precipitate the rise of a new regime to dominance.

Despite the dominance of one trade regime or another during a given period of world history, other regimes may exist. How do we find them? Words are the best evidence of a regime's existence. The articulation of principles, norms, rules, and decision making procedures in documents and in the speeches of representatives and policy makers are *prima facie* evidence of alternative regimes. This book explores and makes sense of these words.

TRADE FLOWS AS EVIDENCE OF REGIMES' EXISTENCE

Other evidence of multiple regimes comes from an analysis of trade flows, though the vast size of the West as both a market and a source for goods makes the interpretation more complex. While it is difficult to use the quantity or direction of trade to identify regimes because regimes deal with the "how" of trade and not the "how much," trade flows provide a rough estimate of the extent of each regime's practices. An analysis of trade flows, which may show a propensity for within regime trading, is further complicated by economic considerations of comparative advantage, proximity, and traditional ties.

I present below some support, in the form of trade data, for the argument that post World War II liberal, Soviet socialist, mercantilist, and South preferential trade regimes have governed international trade. Most industrialized market economy countries support some of the norms or procedures which may be described as mercantilist or post World War II liberal. Simple trade data does not allow the differentiation between trade that is mercantile and trade that is liberal. Many developing countries with market economies follow trading practices which correspond to what I have termed South preferential and/or post World War II liberal practices. Again, trade flows do not differentiate between regimes. Trade among the centrally planned economies is easier to interpret. Most centrally planned economies followed trading practices which corresponded to Soviet socialist trade rules. The chart below shows destination of exports from a particular country group as a percentage of total exports from that particular group.

As the chart shows, both industrialized and developing market economy countries export primarily to the industrialized market economy countries. The low level of South-South trade is likely a function of developing countries' low income and resulting inability to import, as well as traditional ties with formal colonial powers. Most of the North-South trade, like the trade within the North, is conducted under post World War II liberal or mercantile trade rules

Table 1-1. Direction of Trade: Percentages (F.O.B. values)

Exports from			Exports to	
	Year	IMECs	DMECs	CPEs
Industrialized	1965	75%	21%	4%
Market Economy	1970	77	19	4
Countries (IMECs)	1975	70	24	6
	1980	71	23	5
	1985	74	20	5
	1988	77	18	4
Developing Market	1965	71	22	7
Economy Countries	1970	74	20	6
(DMECs)	1975	71	24	5
	1980	70	25	4
	1985	63	28	7
	1988	64	27	8
Centrally Planned	1965	22	14	63
Economies (CPEs)	1970	24	16	57
	1975	27	16	57
	1980	33	18	49
	1985	26	22	51
	1988	25	23	52

(Rows may not total exactly 100% because of rounding.)
Source: UN, *1988 International Trade Statistics Yearbook*

because of the economic dominance of the industrialized countries and because of the relative inability of the Southern countries to implement South preferential trading strategies in the form of commodity arrangements.

Another question here, though, is to what extent do the actual practices of North-North and North-South trade correspond to mercantilist trade as opposed to post World War II liberal trade? This question is more difficult to answer because data on the amount of trade restrained voluntarily or through protectionism are not available. However, voluntary export restraints, orderly marketing arrangements, and protectionist policies have been proliferating in recent years, thus suggesting that mercantilist trading practices are on the rise.

The former strength of the Soviet socialist regime and its recent decline also appears. Although proximity of the Eastern European countries may account for some of the preference for within bloc trade in the 1960s and 1970s, the structure of the regime encouraged within regime trade by using transferable rubles and an account clearing system within CMEA. The proportion of exports from centrally planned economy countries to other centrally planned economy countries dropped from 63 percent in 1965 to a low of 49 percent in 1980. The proportion of trade conducted within the bloc fluctuated between 51 and 55 percent between 1981 and 1988, leveling off to about 52 percent at the end of that period. The disintegration of the Soviet socialist regime should be manifest in further reduction in trade among these countries.

WHAT IS A TRADE DISPUTE?

The preceding discussion has focused on the concept of international regimes. In order to apply this revised theory of regimes to explaining trade disputes, I need to be more precise about what a trade dispute is. As Figure 1-2 illustrates, forms of trade conflict can be seen along a continuum. Latent problems are not articulated by the potential participants (the policy makers of states and of non-state actors such as multinational corporations, producer groups, international organizations, etc.). At the other extreme, trade wars (also called tariff wars) are recognized as exceptionally serious by the policy makers involved. In between are trade problems and trade disputes.

Latent problems exist when the goals of the actors are incompatible but no actor has articulated that incompatibility in any public forum. Competition itself constitutes a latent problem because a sale

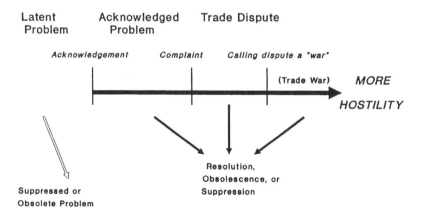

Figure 1-2. Phases of trade conflict

by citizens of one country may well indicate the loss of a sale by citizens of another country. Incompatible policies constitute latent problems when policy makers do not recognize the incompatibilities or do not choose to challenge them.

How, when, and why certain problems are latent and others pass the threshold and become acknowledged are questions of agenda-building. Within states, interest groups that are able to raise their issues to national prominence demonstrate, in doing so, their power. Typically, producer groups are more likely and consumer groups less likely to raise their problems to the public agenda so that policy makers acknowledge them. When policy makers fail to recognize problems, they make "non-decisions."[15] My study of trade conflict begins at this threshold of acknowledging the problem. Once a policy maker has acknowledged through some public forum that the policies of another trader are incompatible and that the other trader is not playing by the rules, then trade conflict exists.

Trade conflict can also be seen as having phases. The mildest form is simply an acknowledged trade problem. In this case, at least one participant has noted the incompatibility but has not expressed a wish that the offending participant change its behavior. A trade problem crosses another threshold and becomes a trade dispute only when at least one participant has noted the incompatible policies in *negative* terms, i.e., its policy makers have made a complaint in a way that can be construed as a call for the offender to change its behavior. The dispute stage encompasses a wide range of trade behavior, including complaints, calls for negotiations, threats, and retaliatory actions. Although most trade is conducted cooperatively, trade disputes are very common occurrences in the international system.

Trade war is a special case of trade dispute. When the policy makers involved in the dispute understand it to be very serious, they call it a trade war. Invoking the metaphor of war has far ranging implications: Here is a trade dispute out of control; here is violence being perpetrated against the economies of the states or financial health of the non-state participants. Often trade wars involve the escalating imposition of tariff and non-tariff barriers to trade (Talbot, 1978; Conybeare, 1985). My impression is that trade wars are becoming more numerous. The frequency with which politicians, business people, and journalists refer to trade war points to the possibility of escalating hostility in any trade dispute.

Figure 1-2 illustrates these phases of trade conflict. Note that at any stage an issue can be suppressed, resolved, or made obsolete.

Each of the phases begins with the crossing of a threshold. The actions which change the relationship from one stage to another are acknowledgement of the problem, complaint about the problem, and speaking of the dispute as a war. Note also that policy makers often choose to acknowledge a problem and make a complaint simultaneously.

REGIMES AND TRADE CONFLICT

How, then, can regimes help explain patterns of trade disputes? Regimes theory focuses the analyst's attention on rules, and conflict can be conceptualized as *behavioral responses to perceived rule-breaking*, in contrast to the rule-ordered behavior of cooperation. The definition has several components. First, what is behavior? In international relations, a state is often thought to have acted or behaved when its army marches. Most international relations, however, involve the representatives of governments saying things to each other. Speech acts are also behavior (Onuf, 1989). Therefore, complaints, requests, threats, and praise, as well as physical acts,are all examples of behavior. This is an important inclusion to bear in mind because trade disputes are conducted primarily at the rhetorical level.

Second, what is a rule? In older works, rules are defined as enforced prescriptions and proscriptions. The role of government as the enforcer of rules within the sovereign state set domestic politics apart from international relations, where there was no enforcement mechanism other than "self-help." A more useful definition of a rule, though, is the more modern approach that identifies rules as shared understandings about what is right and what is wrong. Note that enforcement is divorced from this definition.

Rules are ubiquitous. General rules about the organization of the inter-state system are widely recognized. For example, there is a general proscription against invading a sovereign state, except when the invaded country has done something (such as invading you first) that provides a rationale for your response.[16] States often invade other states, so the rule is often broken. Yet it remains a rule because it is codified in international documents (e.g., the UN Charter) and, more importantly, because it is generally accepted by the people who engage in international relations. When a state does attack without justification, the conflict begins with the victim's response. If a state attacks and meets with no response, then the victim either accepts the justness of the attacker's action or, due to the victim's weakness, is forced to suppress its otherwise preferred responses.

Rules matter because they are the heuristics that make international relations meaningful. Policy makers of states can identify the interests of their states only because rules define the system in which states exist. What is the role of states in the international system? What is good or desirable for a state? What is legitimate or illegitimate behavior? Rules provide the answers. Kegley and Raymond explain:

> [Rules] reflect a set of psychological dispositions fixed within the mind of statesmen. They are produced by a ceaseless, open-ended dialogue in which statesmen appeal to socially recognized interpretive themes, articulate understandings in performing their socially established roles as policymakers, and contribute to the ongoing discourse by which these themes and understandings are affirmed (Kegley and Raymond, 1990: 20).[17]

When a policy maker perceives that a shared rule has been violated, conflict is the result. Defining conflict in terms of perceived rule-breaking stands in sharp contrast to the usual definition of conflict as incompatible interests (Coser, 1956; Snyder and Diesing, 1977; Dahl, 1976, refers to "conflicting aims"). Incompatible interests are endemic to the international system and as such are not useful in identifying instances of conflict. The policy makers of states and other organizations initiate conflict through a behavioral response only when the policy makers perceive that the rival has violated a rule. States almost never declare war for the hell of it. Rather, they claim that their rights (such as their right to sovereignty) have been violated. This speech act is not simply empty and self-serving rhetoric. Rather, this claim has meaning within the context of international relations; it is part of the on-going discourse about the rules and the understandings that policy makers share about them. How states' policy makers justify their actions and defend their rights provides the key to their expectations about what the rules of the game are and how they should be interpreted.

In the case of trade disputes, mercantilist and liberal policy makers often refer to the unfair practices of their trade partners. Unfairness presupposes a standard of fairness ensconced in rules. Soviet analysts have often written pejoratively of interimperialist collusion, which, by implication, is wrong and violates a rule. International traders have very different understandings of what the rules are and what they mean.

In other words, trade rules frame trade disputes. Intersecting sets of rules constitute regimes, and different states and other traders adhere to different regimes. Because the world is composed of groups of actors of contending ideological stripes, behavior in any particular issue may be ordered by more than one regime. Different sets of rules—as well as gaps and ambiguities in the rules or disagreements on the implementation of accepted rules—account for conflict.

Most trade takes place without any of the parties involved voicing opposition to the terms of the transaction or to the way in which the transaction was arranged. A trade dispute, in contrast, represents a departure from this (at least ostensibly) amicable relationship. Trade disputes are the outcome of at least one international actor claiming that the rules of the game for trade have been broken or no longer obtain. Although some may argue that a trade dispute demonstrates that no regime exists, I show that in the current system trade disputes serve to highlight the principles, norms, rules, and decision making procedures of different, contending regimes. The claims and rebuttals made by those participating in the dispute refer to different ideologically coherent sets of rules or different interpretations of the rules. Trade disputes provide an opportunity for actors to articulate their expectations about proper trading behavior.

If multiple trade regimes co-exist, they should be useful for predicting the patterns of trade dispute initiation, process, and outcome. At the broadest level, I suggest that *regimes interact with other political and economic factors to influence actors' perceptions, expectations, and behaviors in the recognition and conduct of trade disputes.*

This hypothesis assumes that international actors behave according to a bounded rationality, though I use the term somewhat differently than Simon (1976). Actors' rationality and probabilistic guesses are bounded not only by uncertainty and complexity, but also by the cultural context of their decision making. Thus actors make a particular judgment of which behavior is most consistent with the micro level factors of their interests, beliefs, feelings, and capabilities. At the macro level, market structure, distribution of power in the international and internal systems, regime structure, and regime strength all affect the micro characteristics.[18]

In the section below, I discuss several propositions about how regimes affect *disputing behavior* (initiation of a dispute, actions taken during a dispute, management and dispute conciliation, and dispute outcomes), *problem recognition*, and *problem interpretation*.

Disputing Behavior (Tested in Chapter 5)

Trade disputes are less likely to break out between adherents to the same regime.

This hypothesis addresses the question of dispute initiation, when a problem becomes a conflict. All else being equal, I expect that trade disputes are less likely to erupt between actors who adhere to the same regime rather than between actors who adhere to different regimes. Trade would tend to be more routinized and rule-governed among members of the same regime.

Once a trade dispute does break out, however, I expect that *(ceteris paribus) disputes within a regime are more easily resolved than disputes involving adherents to different regimes.*

Disputes within a regime are among like-minded actors. They approach the dispute with roughly the same assumptions about the principles and norms of trade. These actors have a stake in upholding their end of what is essentially a bargain with their trading partners. (See Shue, 1986.) In addition, sharing a belief in the principles and norms of a trade regime ought to be associated with many other shared political and ideological values. Actors involved in disputes within a regime are likely to have a high degree of political and cultural affinity which may diffuse economic tensions. Third, actors adhering to the same regime may have had similar disagreements in the past and may have developed a method of resolving the issue before it escalates to trade war. Fourth, the centrality of regime issues to the subject of the case (that is, regime pertinence) should also affect the ease of resolution.

Trade disputes are likely to be less hostile and more cooperative within a regime than across regimes.

The argument for this hypothesis is the same as for the previous one. Shared beliefs are likely to restrain the hostile actions of the participants and encourage cooperative actions aimed at decreasing the levels of hostility of the dispute.

The international political system is ill-equipped for undertaking the kinds of dispute conciliation necessary for resolving trade disputes.

Because there is no universal agreement on principles, norms, rules, procedures, and domains among state and non-state actors, I expect formalized dispute conciliation mechanisms (e.g., the dispute resolution facility of the GATT) to be of limited effectiveness. Formalized dispute conciliation procedures are likely to be most effective in cases involving adherents to the same regime. The facilities for dispute conciliation among adherents to different regimes, in contrast, are *ad hoc*, and the actors engaging in negotiations have fewer values in common. Once again, however, how strongly the participants comply with the regime, coherence of the regime, and pertinence of regime issues may affect the success of dispute conciliation, both within and across regimes.

The outcomes of trade disputes should be more satisfactory to the participants in cases involving adherents to the same regime.

The shared values of adherents to the same regime, along with the existence of dispute conciliation procedures, are more likely to result in a satisfactory outcome than in cases among adherents to different regimes.

Problem Recognition (Explored in Chapters 3, 5, and 6)

The co-existence of four trade regimes is a characteristic of a disorderly, but not anarchical world.[19] We should be able to identify patterns of how trade problems are framed by these regimes.

We should recognize this disorder in the overlapping of rules (Chapter 3), the way trade problems are recognized and described by different sources (Chapter 5), and the way regimes order how cases are similar to each other (Chapter 6).

Sources of information on trade problems, I suggest, are likely to be associated with different regimes. The people who write the reports are themselves members of a society bound by a core ideology. In essence, reporting trade problems is part of the process by which they are socially constructed. The public reporting of trade problems should be related to regime perspectives. In addition, the ways in which cases overlap by commodity, issues, participants, and rules invoked should also reflect the complexity of multiple regime membership and overlapping rules for trade.

Problem Interpretation (Explored in Chapter 4)

Regimes provide the context of trade disputes by filtering the perceptions and interpretations of the participants.

This hypothesis suggests that although economic and political factors may trigger changes in phases of disputes that lead the participants to greater or lesser levels of hostility, regimes are the filters with which actors perceive and interpret these political and economic changes. Thus regimes have value as explanations of why actors pursue certain policies.

These hypotheses, which I test with data on international disputes over trade in food and feed, suggest ways in which regimes may be an important factor—but not the only factor—in determining the patterns of trade disputes. This multiple regime framework includes states, international organizations, firms, and producer groups as participants, although states are the most influential actors. The underlying assumptions of the regimes are explicitly scrutinized. In all, this approach allows us to examine interpretive, as well as causal, questions about how and why regimes are important.

DATA AND METHODS

To support the argument that four regimes have ordered trade in food and feed, I examine 62 food and feed trade problems and disputes which were mentioned in US, EC, Soviet, or UN sources between 1978 and 1983. Seventeen of these cases were simply noted (without coincident complaints) as acknowledged problems in the official documents I consulted, and 45 became disputes (i.e., at least one international actor claimed, in a public arena through official statement or action, that the trade policy of one or more actors violated a rule of international trade). A few of the disputes involved the imposition of a retaliatory tariff or an action of even greater hostility. These eight cases, the most severe among the data I collected, might be considered trade wars.

The analysis includes both qualitative and quantitative approaches to studying food and feed trade disputes that took place between 1978 and 1983. This period is interesting because during it the number of agricultural trade disputes increased and US dominance declined. Also, the US embargo on exports of grain to the Soviet Union in 1980 caused a major perturbation in the agricultural trade system, which led to the further erosion of US domination.

To conduct the analysis, I developed case synopses by combining descriptive material from all the sources reporting on a particular issue. My intent is to limit my own American chauvanism: By combining, rather than interpreting, the descriptions of the issues, I attempt to incorporate the perspectives of officials from different states and international organizations. The sources are: the US Department of Agriculture publication, *Foreign Agriculture*; the *Bulletin of the European Communities*; *Green Europe*, a newsletter of the EC's Common Agricultural Policy; *Activities of the GATT* ; the *Official Records* of the United Nations Commission on Trade and Development (UNCTAD); the UN Food and Agriculture Organization (FAO) publication, *The State of Food and Agriculture*; the Soviet publication, *Foreign Trade*; and information from the clipping files of the US Department of Agriculture Economic Research Service East Europe Division and the library of the European Communities Delegation in Washington, DC.

CAVEATS

The theory and the design of the research are not without limitations. The most obvious defect of a multiple regime theory is that parsimony has been lost. But the world is a complex place, and a correct application of Occam's Razor requires that theory be as simple as possible while still explaining the essential phenomena.

There are other limitations as well. For example, although the framework is the result of an attempt to escape the assumptions of Western liberalism by suggesting that liberalism is not the only ideology having an effect on trade, the way in which I have presented these alternative ideologies and regimes follows a pluralist model, which is itself a liberal construction. I have not escaped the liberal pluralist American political science subculture of which I am a part. The danger is that from a pluralist perspective, it is easy to fall into an assumption that is not necessarily true (or desirable): that each of the regimes is (or should be) as important, strong, or effective as the others.

A constraint on the study is that it relies on public sources of information to define the parameters of the regimes. Although this problem is most evident in the case of the Soviet socialist trade regime, the other regimes are similarly affected. It is possible to gather information on mercantilist trade practices, for example, from a few sources such as official documentation on the Multi-fiber Arrangement negotiations or from testimony by industry representatives before the House and Senate committees on trade. A comprehensive treatment of mercantilist regimes, from the perspective of each of its adherents, not only does not exist, but would be impossible to compile. Moreover, I have not been able to include information from subnational and transnational actors. Data, for example, on disputes between subsidiaries of the same corporation over transfer prices are not available. Much more information from many more sources would be necessary to construct an ideal framework.

These limitations notwithstanding, however, the multiple regime framework is useful because it provides a link between the ideological and political orientation of actors, the rules they develop, and conflict and cooperation.

PLAN OF THE BOOK

In Chapters 2 and 3, I develop a theory by specifying the content of the four contending trade regimes I have identified. I examine the principles, norms, rules, decision-making procedures, formal institutions, codifications of rules, adherents, compliance, and coherence of each regime.

The case study in Chapter 4 takes an in-depth look at regime explanations of the dispute over international sugar trade. In the contention over trade in this commodity all four regimes are represented in the claims made by international actors. The multiplicity of regime-based rules exacerbates the conflict, but the overlapping nature of the rules may provide for future accommodation and unity.

In the fifth chapter, I focus on my data and the results of statistical hypothesis tests. In Chapter 6, I use both discursive and quantitative methods to show how issues and regimes overlap in the cases included in my data. The patterns of rule and norm claims as they frame trade disputes are related to the ideological and political orientation of the participants.

In the conclusion, I examine a world in which hegemony is declining and the effect of these changes on trade regimes. I argue that mercantilism, not liberalism, will emerge as the dominant ideology in the wake of the relative decline of the United States and the collapse of the Soviet bloc.

NOTES

1. From the text of a speech by Edouard Saouma, American University, Washington, D.C., 22 October 1992.
2. Interview, 18 November 1992. Some people I interviewed requested anonymity due to the sensitive nature of their remarks. I have limited identifying information in the text.
3. This study also noted that free trade in wheat and maize might well lead to a net welfare loss for developing countries because most developing countries are net grain importers.

4. Puchala and Hopkins (1982) write of a food regime that incorporates food trade, food aid, and agricultural research. They do not make any references to the GATT.
5. With the notable exception of Young (1980 and 1982) and Aggarwal (1985), most scholars have attempted the "fit" a single regime to all the behavior in an entire issue (or economic sector). Examples include Jervis (1982) and Smith (1987) on a security regime, Zacher (1987) on a commodity trade regime, Dunn (1987) on an automobile trade regime, and Keohane and Nye (1977) on an ocean use regime and a money regime.
6. The importance of the expectations of different groups of actors—and the difficulty of analyzing them—is discussed by Kratochwil and Ruggie (1986). "The emphasis on convergent expectations as the constitutive basis of regimes," they write, "gives regimes an inescapable intersubjective quality" (1986: 764). They call for an interpretive exploration of the "meaning" of regimes, the meaning derived by the participants.
7. Alker (1981) articulated a very similar view. He divided the world into four "partial world orders": capitalist power-balancing, Soviet socialism, corporatist authoritarianism, and collective self-reliance.
8. Contrast Aggarwal (1985), discussed below.
9. Walker (1984) uses this sense. A different, older definition is presented by Mannheim: Ideologies are systems of ideas held by "those strata which represent the prevailing social and intellectual order.... The representatives of a given order will label as utopian all conceptions of existence which *from their point of view* can in principle never be realized" (1936: 196). Crises, according to Mannheim, lead to the development of conservative ideologies and radical utopias, both of which represent distortions of reality and lead to clouded thinking. See also Apter (1964); Johnson (1968); Shils (1968).
10. Other scholars (E. Haas, 1980; P. Haas, 1989; Cowhey, 1990) have stressed the importance of "epistemic communities" in the development of the content of regimes. An epistemic community, a term derived from the sociology of knowledge literature (see Holzner and Marx, 1979), is essentially a group of experts who, through their professional training, come to share assumptions and causal beliefs. Often the reference is to scientists who share a belief in the scientific method. My focus on ideology is consistent with, but more general than, the epistemic community approach. When the nature of the issue area being regulated by the regime is "technical" and requires the input of people with specialized scientific knowledge, then the epistemic community is an important force in the shaping of the regime. The consensual scientific knowledge of the epistemic community is, essentially, its ideology for this specific issue.
11. Zacher, an example of the former, identifies "*the* international commodity trade regime" as a single regime (1987, stress added). An example of the latter is Strange (1982), who challenges the existence of a trade regime by citing the differences in principles and rules for trade between market economies and centrally planned economies.
12. Aggarwal postulates a universal meta-regime or a complex embedded regime for trade, thereby avoiding the problem of the considerable differences in the principles, rules, and procedures of several distinct regimes. For example, until the dramatic changes in the Soviet bloc, the Soviet Union and its allies affirmed principles concerning trade practices which differed greatly from those of the industrialized market economy countries.
13. Keeley (1990) discusses the potential malign characteristics of regimes by analyzing how regimes control power and knowledge, an approach that borrows from the work of Michel Foucault.
14. Rosenau (1990) uses the term, turbulence, differently.

15. See Bachrach and Baratz (1970) on non-decisions in the policy making process; Olson (1971) on interest groups and their political power.
16. Prior to the Treaty of Westphalia, the rules governing the identity of the units of the international (European) system and their behavior were different. Therefore, the nature of conflict—what the participants saw as the contentious issue—was different. As Tetreault notes, "[t]he Westphalian principles of *cujus regio, eius religio* was meant to discourage attempts by European leaders to use religion to justify imperialism against their neighbors (1988: 7).
17. Kegley and Raymond are defining norms, but in this instance the terms are synonymous.
18. Different authors have studied these attributes. Market structure is a concern for those, like Stephen Krasner (1985), who look at how changes in markets affect regime creation and change. The distribution of power in the international system is a focus of those who work within the theory of hegemonic stability (Keohane and Nye, 1977; Lake, 1988) and those who refute it (Russett, 1985, for example). The distribution of power within states is a variable examined by Haggard and Simmons (1987). Several scholars have focused on regime structure and regime strength (e.g., Rothstein, 1977; Keohane, 1984).
19. See Alker (1981). I am using anarchy in the sense of ungoverned. Disorder refers to a partially governed system. An orderly world would be one in which one regime prevails and all activity is performed according to its rules. A disorderly world, in contrast, has many sets of rules. Some behavior abides by the rules of one or other of the sets; other behavior simply breaks rules or is not governed by rules at all. An anarchic world would have no sets of rules.

Chapter 2

Dominant Regimes of the Pre-*Perestroika* Era: Post World War II Liberal and Soviet Socialist Trade

In November 1992, United States Special Trade Representative Carla Hills discussed the possibility that the potential US retaliation against European Community oilseed policies would be met by counter-retaliation. She said:

> Well, it would be totally *illegal* for Europe to have any counter-retaliation. We're moving forward on our GATT [dispute conciliation] panel case that we won, not once, but twice in the last five years, so in effect, we're seeking to *garnish*, to get *restitution* of harm bound to us. Europe doesn't have any such *judgement*. It simply would be acting outside the ambit of *international trade law*.[1] [Stress added.]

"Illegal," "garnish," "restitution," "judgement," "international trade law": These terms all refer to a legal system, to a system of recognized rights and, hence, of rules. The rules that Hills refers to here are the GATT rules that she chose to claim were operative in 1992.

Specific rules, in conjunction with principles, norms, and decision-making procedures, organizations, and foundational documents comprise regimes—regimes that, as in the quotation above, provide claims that are made in the conduct of trade diplomacy. To find the conditions that preceded and prefigured the current situation, I examine the four important regimes of the post War era. What are the actual principles, norms, rules, decision-making procedures, organizations, and documents that constitute these regimes? Who adheres to which regime, to what degree do they comply, and how coherent are the regimes? This chapter and the next answer these questions by systematically analyzing the components of the post World War II liberal trade regime, the Soviet socialist trade regime as it was in the pre-*perestroika* era, the mercantilist trade regime, and the South preferential trade regime. Chapter 2 defines the terms and covers the post World War II liberal and Soviet socialist trade regimes. Chapter 3 continues with the two regimes—the mercantilist and South preferential—that challenge the dominance of the two economic systems that divided the world during the Cold War. Chapter 3 concludes with a discussion of how the rules of the different regimes overlap.

SOME DEFINITIONS

The differences between principles, norms, rules, and decision-making procedures are rather blurry. I follow Keohane, who understands *principles* in terms of the purposes that regime adherents are expected to pursue, *norms* in terms of clarifying what is legitimate or illegitimate behavior, and *rules* in terms of the rights and duties of adherents. Keohane further notes that principles, norms, rules, and decision-making procedures can all be thought of as "injunctions of greater or lesser specificity" (1984: 57–59).

Decision-making procedures, according to Krasner (1982), Keohane (1984), Kratochwil and Ruggie (1986), and others, are the heuristics and institutions, including formal international organizations, that regularize rule-bound behavior. Procedures are better conceptualized as special rules that routinize rule implementation and change. The procedures most interesting from the conflict management perspective of this study are those dealing with dispute argumentation and conciliation, and it is on these that I focus. Although institutions can be conceived as procedures, I think it is more fruitful to look at *formal institutions*, such as international organizations, as separate elements of a regime. In addition, *codifications* of a regime—documents that articulate the principles, norms, rules, and procedures—formalize the regime. Written rules may be available to the public (in the case of regimes whose participants have open societies) or to the appropriate government officials (in cases of regimes including closed societies, particularly the Soviet bloc).

Policy makers who invoke the principles and norms of a regime when they talk about how trade ought to be conducted are the regime's *adherents*. By extension, states (or firms), as organizations of policy makers, can also be considered adherents of regimes. A state may adhere to more than one regime because policy makers may invoke different principles under different circumstances. I interpret regime adherence by looking at the words used by policy makers when they make their normative claims. *Compliance* by the adherents—how closely they abide by the regime's rules—is another important characteristic of the regime to measure.

Coherence refers to two things:

(1) the internal consistency of the principles, norms, rules, and decision-making procedures; and
(2) the extent to which the adherents agree upon the
   (a) rules and
   (b) substantive reach (scope) of the regime.

Internal consistency refers to how well the principles, norms, rules, and procedures are mutually supportive rather than contradictory. Agreement focuses on how stable the regime is. When the adherents agree on the rules and the scope, it is stable. For a regime to exist, there must be broad-based agreement on the principles and norms because disagreement over principles and norms would signify regime decay.[2] In general, a functioning regime's adherents will agree on most of the rules and on the scope.

When are rules or decision-making procedures contended? An established rule may come under fire for no longer being relevant. A new rule or procedure may be proposed, but some participants may not wish it to take effect. Similarly, some participants in the regime may want the scope of the regime to expand or contract. A current example is the Multilateral Trade Negotiation Uruguay Round initiative to expand the post World War II liberal trade regime to include trade in services.

In short, expectations about rules, procedures, and scope, though converging, are not identical. To distinguish between accepted and contended elements of the regime, I refer to the *disputed rules* and the *disputed scope* as those rules and substantive issues which may be evolving into part of the regime or which may be devolving from it. (See Table 2-1.) In the discussion of the specific regimes, I have emphasized the disputed rules and scope because trade disputes often develop over these issues. The identification of disputed rules and scope is one of the most important ways in which regimes can explain conflict.

What follows are the principles, norms, rules, the decision-making procedures, formal institutions, codifications of rules, adherents, compliance, and coherence of each regime, the post World War II liberal and Soviet socialist in this chapter, the mercantilist and South preferential in the next. I put rules that occur in more than one

Table 2-1. Disputed Rules and Scope

	Rules	Scope
Not disputed	accepted rules of the regime's formulation in terms of principles, norms, and rules	commodities/products which are generally considered to be under the regime's aegis
Disputed	rules and decision-making procedures which are not generally accepted by the regime's participants	commodities/products for which the relevance of regime rules is not generally accepted by the regime's participants

regime in the same words each time the rule appears. This intentional redundancy emphasizes how the rules overlap.

I have interpreted the principles, norms, rules, and procedures of each regime from documents that codify them. These documents are distinct from those that I use to provide data on trade problems. Extracting rules from documents and not from observed practices allows me to avoid the tautology of inferring the existence of a regime from behavior and then arguing that regimes order the behavior, a common error pointed out by Haggard and Simmons (1987).

THE POST WORLD WAR II LIBERAL TRADE REGIME

The post World War II liberal trade regime has received the most attention, especially from American scholars. This regime is the most highly structured and widely accepted. Liberalism informs the development of the post World War II liberal trade regime's principles. Liberalism places free trade as the greatest good, yet accepts limited governmental intervention in markets to correct market failures. Market failures and the role of governments in dealing with them are inescapable parts of the contemporary state system. Trade improves welfare, as does the existence of governments, if the governments act prudently. Actors are rational and they wish to maximize their utility.

Principles and Norms

The central principles of the regime are not easy to identify. Robert Keohane (1984: 188–89) lists "non-discrimination, liberalization, and reciprocity" along with preferences for developing countries among the principles of GATT. Carolyn Rhodes identifies the contradictory concepts of efficiency and sovereignty as the central principles, thereby highlighting the underlying tension within the regime. Both efficiency and sovereignty derive from the liberal economic paradigm (Rhodes, 1989).

Efficiency as a central principle reflects the belief that the more freely trade flows, the more utility accrues to traders and consumers. Equity concerns, both domestic and international, are of secondary importance. The principle of sovereignty is embodied in the doctrine that states have a right and a duty to protect their national security, including economic security, a constraint on the free market that was well understood by Adam Smith. The centrality of sovereignty distinguishes the post World War II liberal trade regime from free trade. (See Gilpin, 1987.) In fact, efficiency usually takes a back seat to sovereignty in this regime. For example, the pursuit of economic efficiency was subordinated to the pursuit of sovereign goals when some of the codes adopted during the Tokyo Round of the Multilateral Trade Negotiations permitted discrimination against states that were not GATT members (Keohane, 1984). I suggest that the Tokyo Round codes represent either a redefinition of national security (i.e., more sectors have come to represent vital national interests), or, in the extreme, a break-down of the liberal regime in favor of a mercantilist trade regime.

The primary norms of the post World War II liberal trading regime, as interpreted from the GATT and the statements of representatives of Western countries in the different rounds of the Multilateral Trade Negotiations, include unconditional most favored nation status (MFN, what Keohane, 1984, refers to as "diffuse reciprocity"), reciprocity (Keohane's "specific reciprocity"), and safeguards of vital economic sectors. MFN closely links the principle of efficiency to trading practices because lowering barriers to imports and exports should, according to liberal economic theory, increase welfare.

Reciprocity and safeguards both relate to sovereignty and often work at cross purposes to MFN. Reciprocity puts national interest ahead of pure efficiency by requiring reciprocal reduction of tariffs (Rhodes-Jones, 1986). Nations can thus give concessions to the extent they receive them. Safeguards clauses allow nations to protect domestic producers, especially those deemed necessary to national security (Finlayson and Zacher, 1981). Another norm of this regime is the Generalized System of Preferences (GSP). Although in some ways the GSP can be interpreted as a long term strategy to redress inequitable resource distributions in order to make trade more efficient, concern for welfare in developing countries seems to be the major rationale. Here, rules that have come to be associated with the South preferential trade regime (see Chapter 3) have penetrated the post World War II liberal trade regime.

Rules and Codifications

The articles of the GATT, as well as the later agreements signed by GATT members, contain the most formalized rules of all the regimes I identify. (The small, short form of the rule is the same as that which appears in the summary Table 3-3.) First, here are the post World War II liberal trade rules that do not overlap with the rules of other regimes.

National Treatment. **States shall accord national treatment with respect to internal taxes and regulation of imported products** (GATT Art. III);[3]

Reciprocity. **Tariffs should be removed through a process of reciprocal adjustment** (GATT Preamble; also, see Keohane, 1984, pp. 188–89);

Balance of payments correction. **Trade measures taken to correct balance of payment problems are only allowed in limited cases, with restrictions, and for limited amounts of time** (GATT Art. XII; Tokyo Round Agreement on Trade Measures Taken for Balance-of-Payments Purposes);

Uniform valuation. **Customs valuation should be done on a uniform basis** (GATT Art. VII; Tokyo Round Agreement on Implementation of Art. VII);

Discrimination for national security only. **Governments may discriminate in favor of national suppliers for governmental procurement only in certain circumstances** (Tokyo Round Agreement on Government Procurement);

Limits on import licensing. **Import licensing requirements should not be used as a barrier to trade** (GATT Art. VIII; Tokyo Round Agreement on Import Licensing Procedures);

Limits on technical standards. **Technical standards and regulations should not be used as a barrier to trade** (Tokyo Round Agreement on Technical Barriers to Trade); and

Limits on state trading. **State trading enterprises must act according to international markets and must not use monopolistic tactics** (GATT Art. XVII).

The following rules overlap rules of other regimes.

Limits on export licensing. **Export licensing should not be used to restrain trade** (GATT Art. VIII; *Foreign Trade*, a publication of the Soviet Union, March 1979);

No subsidies. **States should not subsidize exports** (GATT Art. XVI; *Foreign Trade*, May 1978);

No quotas. **There should be no quantitative restrictions on imports or exports** (GATT Art. XI; *Foreign Trade*, February 1978);

Protection of certain sectors. **States (especially major traders) may in given circumstances safeguard economic sectors** (GATT Art. XIX, XX, and XXI; *Arrangement Regarding International Trade in Textiles, 1973* and the *Protocol Extending the Arrangement Regarding International Trade in Textiles, 1981,* commonly referred to as the Multi-Fiber Arrangement, subsequently cited as MFA);

Special rights for LDCs. **Developing countries are to be accorded special rights and are to be exempted from some of the duties required of developed countries** (GATT Generalized System of Preferences; UNCTAD Integrated Program for Commodities; UNCTAD 1979 *Proceedings*, "Document submitted by the Socialist countries," subsequently cited as Document);

Non-discrimination. **States should not apply discriminatory restrictions** (e.g., if a quota is imposed for one of the permitted reasons, the quota should not affect the imports from one country more than the imports from another country; GATT Art. XIII; UNCTAD Secretariat Progress Report on "Protectionism and Structural Adjustment in the Agricultural Sectors"; Document);

Minimum prices. **Minimum prices for some commodities should be established** (Tokyo Round Agreement on Dairy; UNCTAD Integrated Program for Commodities; Document, as implied by support of long term arrangements and market stability); and

No dumping. **Commodities should not be dumped on the international market in an attempt by states or corporations to protect their own economies, gain income, and/or harm the economies of other countries** (GATT Art. VI; implicit in UNCTAD Integrated Program for Commodities; explicit in several bilateral agreements; implicit in Document references to actions by transnational corporations).

Procedures and Formal Institution

Post World War II liberal procedures for conducting trade in accordance with these rules take the form of firms or governments signing contracts to purchase goods or services at market prices. Using the market to the extent possible is a key element of this regime. Other decisions are made by routinized procedures as well. Rounds of Multilateral Trade Negotiations (MTN) provide a method for states to create new rules for trade, change the existing rules, and implement reciprocal reduction of tariffs. Recently, these talks have been used to expand the rules and scope of the post World War II liberal trade regime, particularly with regard to rules for domestic and export subsidies (the Subsidies Code) and the substantive area of agricultural products (the Dairy and Meat Agreements of the Tokyo Round). Uruguay Round discussions have introduced trade in services and intellectual property to the scope of the GATT.

The GATT procedures for dispute conciliation encourage nations first to engage in bilateral negotiations and consultations in order to resolve their differences. If the bilateral negotiations do not result in a mutually acceptable settlement of differences, the GATT Council has the option of invoking two other procedures. The first procedure involves establishing an *ad hoc* working group which includes representatives of the countries involved as well as representatives of other countries. The second procedure, however, has become more common over the years. This method involves establishing an independent panel of experts, none of whom is a national of the countries involved, to study the conflicts and make recommendations.

The process of dispute conciliation within GATT follows a judicial model, and cases before the GATT Council have attributes of a civil suit. In general, a state (the plaintiff) raises a dispute before the GATT Council for conciliation only after bilateral negotiations, as detailed in Articles XXII and XXIII of the GATT, have failed. "Bilateral" is a key term, since under the GATT rubric disputes are conceived fundamentally in terms of Nation A (the claimant or plaintiff) versus Nation B (the defendant). The GATT Council is looked upon as a mediator of last resort, and the entire dispute conciliation process is geared toward encouraging a "private" settlement (akin to settling the matter out of court) between the two parties. Although the GATT allows for working groups to be set up in which the disputing nations can attempt, with an unbiased mediator, to work out an acceptable solution to their disagreement, it has become increasingly common for disputants to request that the Council appoint a panel of experts to study the problem, weigh the arguments of the disputants, and make a report.

An example of this procedure in practice is the case of Chilean complaints over European Community restrictions on exports of Chilean apples. Chile brought its complaint before the GATT Council in 1979, and, in accordance with GATT procedures, Chile and the EC began bilateral consultations. A panel was appointed by the Council after no solution could be found through bilateral negotiations.

While the panel reviews the matter (a process which often takes a year to complete), the disputants usually continue or reopen bilateral negotiations in order to find an acceptable solution. In some instances, the matter is dropped after the two parties have resolved their differences. In other instances, the claimant requests that the panel continue its deliberations to determine exactly what the rights of each party are and to set a precedent for future cases. This latter procedure was followed by Chile in the dispute over its apple exports to the European Community. The panel's report sided with Chile, and both Chile and the EC found the report satisfactory (*Activities of the GATT*, 1980: 49–51). In some cases in which the principal parties to the dispute have settled their differences other nations with similar claims refuse to allow the matter to be dropped. The involvement of these third parties is reminiscent of groups or individuals who file *amicus curiae* briefs in civil court cases. In these cases the Council may continue to discuss the issue and the panel may continue its study of the matter.

The major benefit of having a dispute conciliation mechanism of this sort is that the effect of differences in power are likely to be minimized. Also, the system allows countries to "have their day in court," to air grievances in an international forum. Countries may gain support from like-minded policy makers of other countries. In addition, the relatively time consuming "adjudication" process—panels generally take about a year to report their findings—serves as a "cooling off period," and many disputes are settled bilaterally in the interim.

There are, however, some problems with the judicial model. First of all, some conflicts, such as the dispute over EC sugar subsidies (described in Chapter 4), are not fundamentally bilateral. The GATT Council attempted to divide a single multilateral dispute into separate disputes between the EC and Australia and between the EC and Brazil. Other countries which had similar claims, though, were not satisfied, and a working group dispute conciliation process—a step away from the judicial model—had to be implemented. Also, the GATT system limits participants to nation-states, even though non-nation actors may have an important role in the dispute.

The most serious limitation of this system of dispute conciliation procedures is that the sovereign rights of nations take precedence over conflict resolution goals because GATT recommendations are not binding. Nations frequently ignore or reject the findings of the panel and the recommendations of the Council and persist in the disputed practice. Moreover, "the GATT is an institution . . . that is essentially stacked against developing countries," as a diplomat from the Caribbean noted. The only sanction available in the face of refusal of a GATT member to change its policy are retaliatory tariffs. Developing countries usually have little retaliatory power when facing more prosperous countries.[4] For instance, in 1983 the United States, to oppose the Sandinista Government, imposed restrictions on imports of sugar from Nicaragua. A GATT panel report, adopted by the Council, concluded that the US policy violated the GATT obligation of non-discrimination. The US neither opposed the adoption of the panel's report nor changed its policy (*Activities of the GATT*, 1983). In situations like this, when the offending state does not comply, the only thing that the plaintiff country has gained by taking the issue to GATT is international sympathy.

The GATT secretariat provides the formal institutional basis for these procedures. Although the originally planned International Trade Organization was never completely realized, the GATT secretariat has been a functional substitute. The secretariat furnishes the technical expertise necessary for the dispute conciliation process. In addition, the secretariat reviews the actions of the Council and publishes many documents, including the summary *Activities of the GATT*. The dissemination of information reinforces the regime by making the record of precedents available to policy makers and analysts.

Adherents, Compliance, and Coherence

Which policy makers adhere to the post World War II liberal trade regime can be evaluated by states' GATT membership and by examining policy makers' wording of normative claims about trade behavior. While many states are among the contracting parties to the GATT, states' policy makers may not always advocate policies consistent with GATT rules. Looking at the normative claims made by policy makers provide a more issue-specific clue to regime adherence. Policy makers are implicitly invoking post World War II rules when they speak of:

- Reciprocal reduction of tariffs,
- GATT rules,
- Liberalization,
- Preferences for developing countries (also invoked by adherents to the South preferential trade regime), and
- Protecting important national sectors (also invoked by adherents to the mercantilist regime).

Policy makers of the major industrialized market economy countries make claims that place them within this regime. Policy makers in the United States, for example, have claimed Japan does not live up to its responsibilities of reciprocally removing tariffs in accordance with the GATT. The US threatened to use subsidized exports to counter

Japanese policies. Here, I believe, the US was tacitly acknowledging that subsidies were prohibited under the post World War II liberal trade regime and threatening a defection to mercantilist rules.

Japan also seems to adhere to both mercantilist and post World War II liberal regimes. Although Japan has engaged in the post World War II liberal-oriented Multilateral Trade Negotiations and has agreed to lower its trade barriers, this country still maintains mercantilist-oriented protection of domestic agriculture through restrictions on imports and occasional use of subsidized exports (the latter in the case of rice). Japan justified its actions by claiming the need to protect the domestic market shares of its agricultural producers.

Industry or producer groups, which usually justify their activities from a mercantilist perspective, advocate policies more clearly associated with the post World War II liberal trade regime when they protest the imposition of trade barriers by states and invoke GATT trade rules.

Compliance with this regime is generally quite high. Since most trade interactions in the world are both non-conflictual in nature and among industrialized market economy countries, the vast majority of trade interactions are likely to comply with post World War II liberal rules.

The post World War II liberal trade regime, as the remnant of the old hegemonic order, is quite coherent due to the explicit codification of principles, norms, rules, and procedures within the GATT. That the GATT is referred to by international actors and that these actors participate in negotiations under the GATT umbrella suggests that the post World War II liberal trade regime has an identifiable structure which lends it the relatively strong level of coherence. However, the inconsistencies between rules upholding sovereignty and those upholding efficiency detract from the general coherence.

Yet the very specificity and internal consistency of the regime open the door to disagreement over how the regime should evolve. An examination of GATT documents reveals that the relevant disputed rules and scope of the post World War II liberal regime are quite extensive, and probably cover all trade interactions for the adherents to the regime, given the somewhat precarious balance of sovereignty and efficiency as the central principles.

Particularly likely to be contended are those rules of the regime which represent a departure from the past. Thus the Generalized System of Preferences, though approved in the 1960s, was implemented very slowly. Moreover, the extent of preferences for developing countries is still subject to debate. Other disputed rules include the revocation of tariff bindings[5] (e.g., the EC's discussions of revoking the zero-tariff binding on soybeans) and the determination of whether particular domestic policies (such as the EC's export restitutions) violate GATT rules. The Multi-Fiber Arrangement, which was negotiated partially under GATT aegis, raises questions about how orderly marketing arrangements can be reconciled with GATT norms. In fact, the Multi-Fiber Arrangement can be seen as an abrogation of post World War II liberal trade norms and an embrace of mercantilist trade norms.

Almost all commodities and products traded by states and firms adhering to the post World War II liberal trade regime now at least technically fall within the regime's scope. Until the Tokyo Round, however, this was not the case, as agricultural products were explicitly exempted from the rules. Current subjects of contention, however, still include the extent to which agricultural commodities really can be considered within the regime's scope.

PRE-*PERESTROIKA* SOVIET SOCIALIST TRADE REGIME

In the pre-Gorbachev era, the Soviet socialist order provided the setting for a trading regime that differed dramatically from the post World War II liberal order. This regime was not often discussed in the regimes literature. An exception is the special issue of *International Organization*, edited by Ellen Comisso and Laura D'Andrea Tyson, on the political economy of the Soviet bloc (Spring 1986). Without relying on regime theory terminology, the authors of the special volume address the principles, procedures, and institutions of the Commission for Mutual Economic Assistance (CMEA, also called COMECON) trade. In practice, policy makers of countries participating in this regime primarily articulated the regime's components by condemning capitalist practices rather than by enunciating alternative modes of proper trade. Consequently, the principles, rules, procedures, codifications, and institutions that I ascribe to the Soviet socialist trading regime are, in part, based on interpretive study by a Western observer.

Principles and Norms

The fundamental principle of this regime, according to the rhetoric from the Soviet Union, was a rejection of capitalist modes of trade, which necessarily involve collusion between capitalists and monopolies (Lenin, 1939). Western interpretation suggests that another fundamental principle is the long-term protection of Soviet hegemony over trade relations and division of labor among the Soviet bloc countries (Marrese, 1986).

Both Soviet and Western sources would agree that the primary norm of this regime was state trading. State trading was used to avoid the capitalist modes of trade without losing the benefits of trade. According to socialists, state trading protected against the accumulation of surplus value by capitalist monopolies and the expatriation of low wage countries' wealth. The Western perspective, however, suggests that state trading served to preserve Soviet hegemony over the bloc (Comisso, 1986: 209) by guaranteeing prices and delivery of commodities needed by the Soviet Union, as well as by solidifying intra-bloc cooperation.

State trading was closely tied to centrally planned development strategies. After World War II, Soviet development plans imposed certain patterns of industrial and agricultural production on the Commission for Mutual Economic Assistance (CMEA) members. The patterns of industrialization and growth mandated by the Soviet Union encouraged intra-CMEA trade in preference to extra-CMEA trade.

The predominant system of accounting, based on the transferable ruble—as opposed to hard currency—was a double-edged sword. For one thing, the use of transferable rubles increased the potential ability of the Soviet Union to play an influential role in the trade relations of its CMEA partners since the Soviet Union could insist that accounts be cleared and trade balanced. On the other hand, persistent surpluses in Soviet-East European trade resulted in the Soviet Union acting as an involuntary lender (Lavigne, 1983: 140). The often-cited Soviet subsidy of oil prices paid by its East European trade partners during the energy crisis of the 1970s suggested that the East European countries had some success in "bargaining to exchange 'allegiance' to the Soviet Union for economic subsidization of trade" (Marrese, 1986: 287; also, Comisso, 1986).

To implement the norm of state trading, the participants in this regime condemned capitalist trading practices and, instead, negotiated longterm arrangements (LTAs) between participants. Non-discrimination in access to markets was another articulated norm, but the Soviet Union, at least, seemed to be very discriminatory in its trade policies. Despite Soviet rhetoric about the evils which capitalism perpetrates against the developing world, other Soviet statements have made it clear that the Soviet socialist regime was not equivalent to the social welfare ideals of the Southern order.[6]

Rules and Codifications

Codifications of the Soviet socialist's trade policies can be seen in the 1977 Constitution of the Soviet Union, Part III, Chapter 8, Article 73, which directs that the State shall conduct all international trade; in certain long-term arrangements which were agreed to among Communist bloc states and between Communist bloc states and the non-Communist bloc states; and in documents submitted by Soviet bloc countries to international conferences. One document, which was submitted to the UNCTAD 1979 Conference, explicates Soviet socialist rules quite plainly.

The Conference documents are especially interesting because they present detailed responses to the international political economy as seen from the Socialist perspective. The documents stressed the culpability of the capitalist world for the situation in the socialist and developing countries and the need for a "radical restructuring of the existing international economic order with due regard for the interests of all groups of countries on equitable and democratic principles" in order to curtail market domination by capitalist countries (UNCTAD, *1979 Proceedings*: 181).

The rules unique to this regime include the following.

Controls on monopolies. **Monopolies should be prevented from controlling the market** (Lenin, 1939; Document);

Controls on capitalist states. **States should not cooperate with and support monopolies' efforts to control the international market** (Lenin, 1939);

State ownership. **States should consolidate national sovereignty over resources and restrict the operations of transnational corporations** (Document); and

State monopoly on trading. **International trading should be done on the basis of state monopoly** (Soviet Constitution).

Soviet socialist rules that overlap with rules from other regimes include:

Limits on export licensing. **Export licensing should not be used to restrain trade** (GATT Art. VIII; *Foreign Trade,* a publication of the Soviet Union, March 1979);

No subsidies. **States should not subsidize exports** (GATT Art. XVI; *Foreign Trade,* May 1978);

No quotas. **There should be no quantitative restrictions on imports or exports** (GATT Art. XI; *Foreign Trade,* February 1978);

Longterm purchase arrangements. **States should make long term purchase arrangements** (MFA; Document);

Special rights for LDCs. **Developing countries are to be accorded special rights and are to be exempted from some of the duties required of developed countries** (GATT Generalized System of Preferences; UNCTAD Integrated Program for Commodities; Document);

Non-discrimination. **States should not apply discriminatory restrictions** (e.g., if a quota is imposed for one of the permitted reasons, the quota should not affect the imports from one country more than the imports from another country; GATT Art XIII; UNCTAD Secretariat Progress Report on "Protectionism and Structural Adjustment in the Agricultural Sectors"; Document);

Minimum prices. **Minimum prices for commodities should be established** (Tokyo Round Agreement on Dairy; UNCTAD Integrated Program for Commodities; Document, as implied by support of long term arrangements and market stability); and

No dumping. **Commodities should not be dumped on the international market in an attempt by states or corporations to protect their own economies, gain income, and/or harm the economies of**

other countries (GATT Art. VI; implicit in UNCTAD Integrated Program for Commodities; explicit in several bilateral agreements; implicit in Document references to actions by transnational corporations).

Procedures and Formal Institutions

The pre-Gorbachev Soviet socialist regime's operation was evident in procedures implemented by the members of the Soviet bloc and in the institution of the Commission for Mutual Economic Assistance. Procedures for socialist trade involved state-state negotiations on prices, quantities, delivery dates, and length of agreements, according to Soviet sources.

The existence of CMEA as an international institution in which Soviet bloc countries participated and through which the terms of trade between bloc members were set demonstrated that a Soviet socialist trade regime existed. In specific terms of dispute conciliation procedures, there is evidence that discussions within the Commission for Mutual Economic Assistance considered problems of intra-Soviet bloc trade. A 1975 meeting of the Executive Committee of CMEA dealt with how to set intra-bloc prices (Lavigne, 1983: 136). Western views are that the autonomy of the Soviet Union's CMEA partners to negotiate freely was limited (Matusek, 1981:101; Laux, 1981).

Adherents, Compliance, and Coherence

The adherents of this regime traditionally were the members of the Soviet bloc, although some of the countries attempted to straddle market economy and centrally planned economy systems. In the wake of the disintegration of this system, it is especially important to look at the kinds of claims made by policy makers who operated within the Soviet socialist trade regime because the routines of trade practices can help predict the direction of future changes. The most common phrases used by Soviet socialist policy makers to make normative claims about trade practices were:

- Exploitation by capitalist monopolies and
- Interimperialist collusion.

Until recently, the dominant position of the Soviet Union within its bloc created a regime in which the rules were obeyed much more closely than in the post World War II liberal regime. Looking at the 1978–1983 period of this study, the Soviet Union strongly adhered, at least in terms of its rhetoric, to socialist trade practices. However, the Soviet Union did trade with multinational corporations, which it denounced as imperialist monopolies. Nevertheless, within CMEA trade conformed to socialist methods because the Soviet Union was able to maintain its hegemonic status over its allies.

Soviet socialist trade, like post World War II liberal trade, was a highly internally consistent regime because of the programmatic nature of Soviet socialist rules. Since the Soviet Union was able to dictate trade practices of its partners, the trade relations of the CMEA countries were clearly defined.

The other measure of coherence, the degree to which the rules and scope of the regime was disputed, suggests an interesting contrast between public statement and private politics. Prior to Gorbachev's changes, official Soviet bloc sources would have denied the existence of contention about the rules or scope of the regime. By socialist definition, trade disputes only occur when the capitalist countries or the international monopolies disrupt true socialist trade. Nevertheless, the record shows discord among socialist trading partners. The disputed rules of the regime included pricing policies and subsidization, the refusal of the Soviet Union to pay in hard currency for most commodities, the length of and negotiation procedures for the longterm arrangements, and the ability of CMEA members to trade with non-CMEA countries. As for the scope, oil and arms may have been the two most disputed commodities. Agricultural products were the subject of dispute primarily in terms of how many barrels of oil a CMEA country could buy with a given quantity of an agricultural commodity. It is also possible that the Eastern European countries resented the preferential agreements, often involving agricultural products, which they were required to enter into with the developing CMEA countries.

* * *

These two regimes represented the two major poles of a bifurcated world. Now, both the post World War II and Soviet socialist regimes have changed, the Soviet trade regime in a more revolutionary manner. The next chapter continues with a discussion of the two regimes that challenge the assumptions and values of the old.

NOTES

1. Carla Hills, interviewed on National Public Radio *Morning Edition*, 10 November 1992.
2. In contrast, Haas (1983) specifies declining coherence and effectiveness of the regime as signs of decay.
3. The citations for the rules provide examples of their codification and do not represent the only sources where the rules may be expressed.
4. Interview, 25 November 1992.
5. A tariff binding is an agreement to set a tariff at a certain level, often in exchange for reciprocal concessions from trading partners. A zero-tariff binding means that the country has agreed not to impose any tariff on a particular good.
6. See also Cutler (1983) on East-South relations at UNCTAD.

Chapter 3

The Challengers: Mercantilist and South Preferential Trade Regimes

"In Europe," an American official opined, "there's an emotional attachment to the land. In Germany it's not uncommon for a family to say that it has worked a piece of land for two hundred or three hundred years . . . . This emotional attachment was reinforced by the wars, when people survived because they were sent to the country. The farm is seen as a security reserve."[1] Linking the ability of farms to survive, implicitly by profitable trading, with a nation's security is the key to a mercantilist approach to trade. The South preferential approach calls upon a different face of security: the security that comes from improved social welfare. In arguing for preferential agreements, a diplomat from the Caribbean put it this way: "The trading system needs a greater sense of empathy and recognition that in the long run we'll all be better off" if the rules redress the unfairness of the current trading system.[2]

These two regimes—the mercantilist and the South preferential— are not as strong as the previously discussed regimes. The mercantilist and South preferential trade regimes are not as institutionalized, do not have the internal consistency, have more areas about which the regime adherents disagree, and do not command the same degree of compliance as the post World War II liberal and Soviet socialist regimes.[3]

These regimes, though, present challenges to the regimes that have dominated since the end of World War II. In particular, both the mercantilist and South preferential regimes are reactions to the dominant post World War II liberal regime. At the same time, the mercantilist and South preferential regimes provide an implicit challenge to Soviet socialism because these challengers' adherents rejects the traditional radical alternative (if you will pardon the oxymoron) to capitalism. Despite their weaknesses, I argue in this chapter, mercantilist and South preferential trading can be considered regimes because they are constituted by rules grounded in ideology.

MERCANTILIST TRADE REGIME

As a regime, today's version of mercantilist trade involves the negotiation or bargaining by states and other legitimated non-state actors (common markets, such as the EC, multinational corporations) to order trade in a manner which is increasingly noncompetitive and "managed."[4] The mercantilist order legitimates the pursuit of wealth as national policy. Participants in this regime articulate the goals and needs of their constituencies. The bargaining for rights to market shares and the pursuit of economic nationalist goals (Gilpin, 1987) has little in common with the ideological underpinnings of liberal efficient competition.

Interest Group Pluralism, Corporatism, and Mercantilist Trade

A mercantilist trade regime is the result of the increasing importance of interest groups in the policy making process. This occurs in pluralist societies in which non-compulsory groups lobby governments and in corporatist societies in the advanced industrial democracies and newly industrializing countries (Schmitter, 1979; Lowi, 1979; Katzenstein, 1984). Olson (1982) argues that interest groups in pluralist societies can hamper efficiency and progress by convincing governments to implement policies that help particular groups. In corporatist societies, the relationship between interest groups and governments is more formal. Schmitter defines corporatism as "a system of interest representation," archetypically one in which the organizations representing the interests are

- (a) singular,
- (b) compulsory,
- (c) noncompetitive,
- (d) hierarchically ordered,
- (e) functionally differentiated,
- (f) recognized, licensed, or created by the state, and
- (g) the only legitimate voice of their members; yet
- (h) controlled by the state (1979:13).

In the Newly Industrialized Countries, corporatism follows a different track, but this corporatism also merges with mercantilism. The eager participation of the NICs in a mercantilist system is a consequence of the state corporatism which reflects the "rapid demise of nascent pluralism" (Schmitter, 1979: 23) within them. NICs' development strategies generally include government intervention in the economy through preferential taxation, subsidies, or other measures. Privileges granted to some sectors at the expense of others are even less problematic in the NICs than in the advanced industrialized democracies because intervention is seen as a legitimate task for government.

In pluralist advanced industrialized societies such as the United States, interest groups are not controlled by the state, nor are they compulsory. Nevertheless, in both the advanced industrialized and newly industrialized corporatist societies and the pluralist societies where interest groups play a large role, the state provides the forum in which interests are articulated. Often the state mediates among the conflicting demands of different groups. Mercantilism is the external manifestation of this system. Policy makers promulgate trade policies which provide advantages to those interest groups, particularly ones that occupy a privileged place in the domestic pecking order.

When the international economy is growing rapidly, mercantilist policies are not necessary because unsuccessful competitors in one market can simply sell elsewhere. However, when competition in international markets is especially intense, trade policies provide a politically expedient way to provide advantages to domestic interest groups: The benefits accrued are direct and immediate, while the costs are diffuse. The interest group receiving the protection immediately sees its situation improve. The people who pay the price tend to be domestic consumers and foreign firms. Foreign firms have little ability to engage in the kind of politicking that got the domestic firms their protection in the first place. Consumers are so inchoate a group that they are usually unable to organize their own interest group. (See Olson, 1971.)

The rise of modern mercantilism is a delayed outcome of the erosion of the post World War II liberal international economic order in developed and developing countries, brought on by the slowing down of economic growth. After World War II, external markets were something of an expanding pie. The international economy was growing so rapidly that externally oriented economic activity did not require bargaining among states for market shares. As the international economy took a downturn in the 1970s, mercantilist policies became more attractive tools to policy makers.

The mercantilist trade regime is associated with the ideology of mercantilism and the pursuit of self-interest by groups. Mercantilism and realism are really two sides of the same coin: Mercantilism glorifies the pursuit of national objectives through the accumulation of wealth; realism does the same through the accumulation of power. The problem, according to liberal economic theory, is that mercantilism is not efficient, its policies—while increasing the wealth of some sectors—do not necessarily increase *national* wealth. To the mercantilist, however, increasing the wealth of important groups within the society is the key criterion for good policy. "Who gets what?" is the key political question. Mercantilist policies increase the wealth of the groups that "count." Which groups count is mediated by the corporatist decision-making process within the society.

Mercantilism, then, is a repudiation of market capitalism (though not of the profit motive). Policy makers wish to provide privileges to some sectors, not necessarily those privileged by the market. In those sectors in which policy makers would prefer to rely on the mechanism of the market, market failures and inefficiencies become increasingly prevalent. In this vein, Seabold and Onuf (1981) identify what they term "international corporatism" (practices consistent with what I term mercantilism) with the devolution of capitalism. These authors define international corporatism as the set of foreign economic policy behaviors originating with late capitalism and the decline of the domestic economies of advanced states. My argument goes a step further. In the emergence of modern mercantilism we see the convergence of the trends toward the increasing importance of interest groups with the trend of increasing competition for market shares in a world no longer dominated by the US economy.

Principles and Norms

In short, mercantilism and the mercantilist trade regime are outgrowths of demands for sovereignty (i.e., legitimate articulation of the needs of the state) and protection of domestic industry (i.e., legitimate articulation of the needs of an interest group within the state) superceding liberal concerns about efficiency. Mercantilism is emphatically not the sort of protectionism associated with the corrections to the market sanctioned by the post World War II liberal regime. (See Ruggie, 1982.) Rather, the mercantile trade regime sanctions the active intervention of states into markets through bargaining over rights to market shares in support of corporatist collectivities.

As the US and other Western countries began to lose their hegemonic power over the international trade system, internal interest groups have argued more and more strongly for regulation of markets through intervention in order to protect the interests of certain sectors. Olson (1982) suggests that political and economic stability within a country gives the interest groups more power because their members have a tradition of coalition building. Groups have created a normative context in which the international bargaining embodies "fair," rather than "free" trade as the ideal.

Just as corporatism cuts across many different substantive and functional areas (Schmitter, 1979: 28), mercantilism is rarely adopted by a nation-state as an economy-wide policy. Rather, certain sectors or issues are highlighted by the agenda-building process within the country. For instance, some groups, such as farm lobbies in industrialized countries, have traditionally been able to exert a good deal of influence on policy making. As the traditional power structure of the international trade system is being eroded, these groups have often advocated a departure from free trade practices.

The mercantilist trade regime can be called a "conservative" regime because it has market stability and the institutionalization of present-day (or the restoration of prior) power hierarchies within the market as its central principles. In contradistinction to the post World War II liberal trade regime, discrimination is a central norm of the mercantilist regime because certain states are to be targeted as threats to market stability and hierarchy. From a corporatist perspective, discrimination corresponds to the interest aggregation and internal control structures of organizations (Staber, 1987: 279) within corporatist states. At the state level, corporatist organizations negotiate on behalf of their members. In foreign economic policy making, states serve to aggregate interests and pursue political negotiations for trade on behalf of exporter and sectoral groups. In contrast to the individual firm as the major actor in a liberal order, the state internally decides which interests to focus on in international negotiations. International organizations such as the European Community or the African, Caribbean, and Pacific states (ACP) may also serve to aggregate the interests of states by implementing discriminatory "deals." Large multinational corporations may have the resources to negotiate in a similar manner to pursue the interests of their shareholders.

Rules and Codifications

The rules which I was able to discern from the mercantilist trade regime are less well organized, primarily because each particular agreement embodies a unique set of requirements. No wide-ranging codification of this regime exists, though all of these arrangements instiutionalize government intervention in a way that reifies the differentials in market power of participating states. Each time the policy makers adhering to this regime conclude a bargain, the agreement codifies the rules. However, no GATT-like systematic framework exists because each mercantilist negotiation targets a separate product. As such, mercantilist agreements are a repudiation of the General Agreement on Tariffs and Trade, which purports to order all trade.

Mercantilist rules can be inferred from an examination of the existing arrangements. Rules that are unique to the mercantilist trade regime include:

Discrimination. **Bilateral and multilateral measures to systematically discriminate against certain (generally Southern) countries** (Multi-Fiber Arrangement; inferred from procedures of voluntary export restraints).

Rules which overlap with other regimes include the following.

Protection of certain sectors. **States (especially major traders) may in given circumstances safeguard economic sectors** (GATT Art. XIX, XX, and XXI; MFA).

Longterm purchase arrangements. **States should make longterm purchase arrangements** (MFA; Document);

Export quotas. **Export quotas (minimum and/or maximum) should be used to stabilize international trade** (MFA and Lomé Convention; UNCTAD Integrated Program for Commodities; inferred from the practices of the Japanese-US voluntary export restraint agreements); and

No dumping. **Commodities should not be dumped on the international market in an attempt by states or corporations to protect their own economies, gain income, and/or harm the economies of other countries** (GATT Art. VI; implicit in UNCTAD Integrated Program for Commodities; explicit in several bilateral agreements; implicit in Document references to actions by transnational corporations).

Procedures and Formal Institutions

The bargaining of compromises (equitable or imposed) is the most common procedure of this regime. This procedure routinizes trade transactions, creates new rules, and allows for the resolution (or management) of disputes. The negotiations may be either multilateral or bilateral. The results of these negotiations are often "voluntary export restraints" (VERs) or "orderly marketing arrangements" (OMAs) which serve to manage the market. Aggarwal (1983; 1985) discusses the Multi-Fiber Arrangement as a failure of liberal trade rules, but the agreement is better identified as an outgrowth of mercantilist rules. Other mercantilist instruments, such as the US-Japanese agreement on restricting Japanese automobile exports to the US, have been bilateral. The specifics of a particular bargaining outcome are codified on an *ad hoc* basis in these agreements. The emphasis is not on unilateral imposition of tariffs or other barriers to trade.

In a different context, Aggarwal, et al. (1987) refer to this new method of trade management as "cooperative protectionism." Strange (1985) argues that bilateral agreements among trading partners have actually helped maintain levels of international trade, despite the recession of the 1980s. The view taken here of such mercantilist trading practices is, admittedly, less sanguine.

At times, the GATT has, ironically, become the institutional home of this regime. The inclusion of the Multi-Fiber Arrangement under the GATT umbrella shows how the organization is maleable and can be coopted for non-liberal purposes. In general, though, no single, formal, universal organization serves to institutionalize this regime because the regime itself is one of organized "deal cutting." States or groups of states can cooperate to aggregate interests and provide a unified voice for the bargaining. No supranational authority exists to mediate among interests. By default, then, the hierarchy of power in markets is reinforced. The regime may be analogous to a balance of power security regime which relies on states' involvement and cooperation (Jervis, 1982).

Adherents, Compliance, and Coherence

Adherence to this regime is most evident among the advanced industrialized countries. The European Community's justifications of the Common Agricultural Policy (i.e., the need to enable EC farmers to sell in world markets) and the policy itself suggest that the EC is primarily an adherent to mercantilist principles, norms, rules, and procedures. The Lomé Convention, however, provides an interesting paradox. Although the rhetoric surrounding the agreement suggests that the rules of the accord are South preferential, the actual rules contained in the Convention serve to manage the market to the advantage of the EC. (See Chapter 4.) Thus the Lomé Convention corresponds to mercantilist rules rather than South preferential ones. Other statements by EC officials suggest that this bloc also complies with post World War II liberal rules. In many cases, the particular regime adhered to depends on the commodity or issue in question.

Compliance, in the case of this regime, is difficult to judge. The Organization of Petroleum Exporting Countries, an organization which certainly represents the mercantilist division of the oil market, seems to have a good deal of trouble maintaining compliance. The 1990 invasion of Kuwait by Iraq began, in part, as a dispute over how much oil Kuwait was supposed to export under OPEC rules. On the other hand, the Japanese successfully placate the Americans through the use of Voluntary Export Restraints.

The phrases that signal adherence the mercantilist regime include:

- Fair trade,
- Protecting market shares, and
- Protecting important national sectors (also invoked by Post World War II liberal adherents).

The lack of coherence in the mercantilist trade regime, I believe, can be attributed to its sector-specific orientation. Although there are principles uniting the perceptions of all adherents to this regime across the specific agreements of the regime (i.e., market hierarchies should be maintained or regained and traditional market shares are "proper"), a particular interest group advocates protectionist policies only to benefit the sector it represents. Thus the mercantilist trade regime reflects an "every state or corporate group for itself" attempt at restructuring economic relations in a time of declining hegemony and power.

The disputed rules and scope of mercantilist trade are many and broad. In terms of rules, how and when (but not if) domestic producers are to be protected is the subject of contention. The degree to which the economies of other nations must be taken into consideration is another rule which may provoke dispute within the regime. In terms of the scope, which products or commodities deserve protection may be disputed. Whether the actor is a nation-state or not, a problem of slow growth, loss of international market share, loss of domestic market share, or any other issue can serve as a trigger to put the problem on a trader's agenda.

Is This a Regime?

Two objections can be raised regarding the validity of a mercantilist trade regime. First, regimes are evidence of cooperation among states and other participants in the international political economy (Keohane, 1984), but the mercantilist trade regime may disadvantage some. My response is that despite the positive connotation of the word, "cooperation," cooperation in this context refers to policy coordination rather than harmony of interests. (I follow Keohane's distinction between cooperation and harmony here.) Regimes need not be beneficial to all, nor even simply not malign. Nothing in the definition of regime as put forth by Krasner and his colleagues speaks to the intentions—for good or evil—of the regime's creators.

The second objection pertains to what exactly constitutes a regime. All those not taking the broadest possible view of the nature of a regime (what has been called the Grotian approach) require more than cooperation and patterned behavior as evidence of a regime's existence. Haggard and Simmons prefer a definition of regimes emphasizing "multilateral agreements among states which aim to regulate national actions within issue-areas" (1987: 495). This definition makes a regime virtually synonomous with a multilateral agreement. Haggard and Simmons would define the Multi-Fiber Arrangement as *a* regime. However, several specific regimes identified with multilateral agreements of the kind fitting Haggard and Simmons' criteria may have the same underlying ideology and principles. When specific agreements (alternatively, regimes with small scopes) are tied together by their ideology and principles, then the regimes are "nested," to use Aggarwal's term, in a superordinate regime (in this case the mercantilist trade regime).

SOUTH PREFERENTIAL TRADE REGIME

Developing country advocates of significant changes in the structure of the international economy have constructed, albeit with questionable success, another trade regime. One ideology behind the Southern order, of which the South preferential trade regime is a part, is social welfare theory. According to the ideology, society—in this case global society—has the responsibility to help the disadvantaged.

Writers invoking this tradition have included Murphy (1984) and Laszlo, et al. (1978). Laszlo, et al., for example, argue that "a transfer of some of the excess wealth of the rich countries to relieve the worst of the deprivation in the many poor ones would be by no means offensive to an informed sense of justice and an enlightened morality" (1978: xxi). They substantiate this claim by citing Rawls's *A Theory of Justice.* Although Rawls chooses not to identify his ideas with the term welfare (because of utilitarian connotations of the term), his emphasis on the criteria of fairness in the political economy coincides with the emphasis of social welfare theory. Fairness depends not on the status quo, but rather on an ideal sense of distributive justice (Rawls, 1971: 258-65).

Murphy, who takes a different tack, stresses the development of the New International Economic Order ideology as a response to the failures of the Bretton Woods system. In this way, the development of the South preferential trade regime parallels the development of the mercantilist trade regime. Both are reactions to problems of post World War II liberal trade. Murphy contrasts the post World War II liberal trade regime's emphasis on property rights with the NIEO's emphasis on

(1) "international management of the global economy,"

(2) "the economic rights and duties of states,"

(3) "the equality of individual states,"

(4) the moral obligation of past and present exploiters to negotiate the reform of the existing international economic systems, and

(5) "the duty of current exploiter states to compensate their victims" (1984: 158).

Each of these points reflects the welfare needs of developing countries. Each argues for the implementation of redistributive justice. (Compare Lowi, 1979: 273-74.)

Principles and Norms

The fundamental principles of the South preferential trade regime reflect the ideals of social welfare theory by attempting to create a stable economic environment—a goal which sounds surprisingly similar to that of the mercantilist trade regime. However, the character of the stability which the South preferential trade regime adherents seek necessarily rejects the status quo. Adherents of this regime seek to redistribute wealth and power among the nations of the world to provide a more equitable allocation. The South preferential trade regime would establish international market rights and duties for countries, depending on their historical economic and political status. This regime embodies the hope for a trading system with predictable prices, demand, and supply of commodities, as well as redistributive justice.

The norm of regulating international markets to create trade rights and to redistribute wealth and privileges fosters equity and stability, according to the adherents to this regime. Commodity agreements are considered the most appropriate way of achieving this regulation. In contrast to the mercantilist trade regime, trade rights under the South preferential trade regime do not favor traditional market shares, but rather favor the counterfactual situation of what the market share would be if this were a fair world. In addition, wealth and privileges must be redistributed in order for Third World countries to acquire (what they consider to be) their rightful position in the international economy.

Rules and Codifications

Formal, specific rules depend on the particular issue, but import and export quotas, as well as internationally or nationally held reserves or other mechanisms are to be used to create stable conditions of supply, demand, and prices. One more rule applies after the special rights of developing countries have been put into practice: No discrimination in access to markets should be applied. In a sense, "positive" discrimination designed to help developing countries is mandated, while "negative" discrimination which could hurt these countries is prohibited.

Import quotas. **There should be minimum import quotas for commodities** (International Sugar Agreement); and

Buffer stocks. **States should contribute to international buffer stocks or other mechanisms to maintain stable prices** (inferred from several commodity agreements being negotiated under the UNCTAD Integrated Program for Commodities).

Rules shared by other regimes include the following.

Export quotas. **Export quotas (minimum and/or maximum) should be used to stabilize international trade** (MFA and Lomé Convention; UNCTAD Integrated Program for Commodities; inferred from the practices of the Japanese-US voluntary export restraint agreements);

Special rights for LDCs. **Developing countries are to be accorded special rights and are to be exempted from some of the duties required of developed countries** (GATT Generalized System of Preferences; UNCTAD Integrated Program for Commodities; Document);

Non-discrimination. **States should not apply discriminatory restrictions** (e.g., if a quota is imposed for one of the permitted reasons, the quota should not affect the imports from one country more than the imports from another country; GATT Art. XIII; UNCTAD Secretariat Progress Report on "Protectionism and Structural Adjustment in the Agricultural Sectors"; Document);

Minimum prices. **Minimum prices for commodities should be established** (Tokyo Round Agreement on Dairy; UNCTAD Integrated Program for Commodities; Document, as implied by support of long term arrangements and market stability); and

No dumping. **Commodities should not be dumped on the international market in an attempt by states or corporations to protect their own economies, gain income, and/or harm the economies of other countries** (GATT Art. VI; implicit in UNCTAD Integrated Program for Commodities; explicit in several bilateral agreements; implicit in Document references to actions by transnational corporations).

Procedures and Formal Institutions

The procedures of this regime are multilateral for both philosophical and pragmatic reasons: Philosophically, to be truly successful, a South preferential trade regime requires the participation of all states; pragmatically, the advocates of the regime are weak and seek strength in numbers. Disputes over rights, duties, and prices are negotiated in multilateral or international fora such as the commodity agreement commission and UNCTAD meetings. The actors shun bilateral arrangements because of their exclusive nature. Moreover, negotiations under this regime are sector or issue specific. Thus separate agreements are negotiated for each of the different commodities included under the umbrella of the Integrated Program for Commodities (IPC). A final distinctive feature of the procedures of the South preferential trade regime involves the venue for negotiations. Most negotiations take place under the aegis of international organizations, the secretariats of which often act as advocates of the principles of this regime.

The New International Economic Order is the main codification of the principles and rules of this regime, and the Brandt Commission Reports (1980 and 1983) remain the quintessential explications of the relationship between social welfare ideology and the practices desired by the participants. UNCTAD and the FAO serve, like GATT for the post World War II liberal trade regime, as the formal institutions for this regime. The role of the UNCTAD and FAO secretariats is essential to the development of NIEO. The secretariats, as advocates for the developing countries, have promulgated reports which point out how market problems affect developing countries. (See, for example, UNCTAD Trade and Development Board document TD/B/885, 18 February 1982.)

Like the GATT secretariat, UNCTAD's and FAO's secretariats disseminate information. Unlike the GATT secretariat, however, these UN organizations' reports and the good offices of their officials seem to be especially "political." The choice of subjects for reports and administrative action, as well as the tone of reports, seem to indicate that these secretariats are actively lobbying for acceptance of redistributive principles. Murphy (1984) suggests that the NIEO involves a political alliance between developing countries and international organizations.[5] Because of the welcoming environment of UNCTAD and other UN agencies, participants in this regime have chosen to promulgate the regime's rules by trying to create commodity agreements under the aegis of these international organizations.

Adherents, Compliance, and Coherence

Many developing countries advocate in public the principles described in the South preferential trade regime, yet real disparities of power may lead them to accept mercantilist or post World War II liberal trade arrangements with more powerful partners.

The words that signify adherence to this regime include:

- Preferences for developing countries (also invoked by post World War II liberal adherents),
- Rights of developing countries, and
- Multilateral regulation of trade.

Compliance with the rules of this regime is low among the adherents. The general weakness of the developing countries that would choose to advocate these rules leads their policy makers to defect to other regimes as necessary. The exigencies of placating a domestic population today may influence policy makers' decisions to abrogate commodity export quotas that would have a benefit in the long run. Also, the pressure that more powerful countries can use against the developing countries may at times lead to defection.

Coherence in the South preferential trade regime suffers from the inability of developing countries to agree on unified policies for all trade. As with the mercantilist trade regime, each commodity is dealt with by a separate arrangement. In the South preferential trade regime case, these arrangements are the individual commodity agreements being negotiated under the Integrated Program for Commodities (IPC). In contrast to the mercantilist trade regime, however, the IPC does offer an umbrella which signals a unity of purpose, if not of practice, among the commodity agreements. Yet the South preferential regime is further weakened by the developing countries' lack of power. As Rothstein (1984) quite correctly points out, the developing countries were largely unsuccessful in creating a New International Economic Order.

The disputed rules and scope of the South preferential regime are well demarcated. The way in which preferences should be formulated and implemented provides the major issues over which there is disagreement regarding the rules. Some of the major questions on the issue of structuring preferential commodity agreements include: How will commodity buffer stocks be financed; who is to hold the buffer stocks; should there be buffer stocks, export/import quotas, or both; what price levels should serve as upper or lower bounds?

The commodities and products that are a part of the disputed scope are primarily those that are either

(a) resources which can be considered "essential" and which therefore can be considered national security issues, especially for cash and resource poor developing countries; or

(b) exports that are essential sources of income for poorer countries.

Although cocoa is not an important food commodity in itself, the revenue which it brings to the Ivory Coast and Ghana is important to the welfare of those countries. Contention surrounds which of the many commodities and products that are necessary either as exports or imports should fall under the jurisdiction of the regime.

Is This a Regime?

Can South preferential trade be considered a regime when its effect on international behavior is so limited? Rothstein (1984) describes the failure of the Group of 77 to create this regime. However, in terms of understanding the claims of international actors in trade disputes, the norms and principles of redistribution, guaranteed access to markets, infant industry protection, etc. which serve to redress the grievances of Third World countries against the industrialized countries, this regime is still salient. Again, the issue is not only whether a regime provides objective limits to the behavior of international actors, but also whether the international actors make claims which refer to a given model of what constitutes proper or improper trade behavior. The South preferential trade regime is, in many respects, an example of an ineffective regime. It has had little behavioral impact because it has not attracted powerful enough adherents. On the other hand, the principles, norms, and rules of this regime pervade the discourse on international agricultural trade in United Nations fora. As an internally consistent, programmatic set of trade rules, the South preferential trade regime presents a challenge to the dominant post World War II liberal trade regime.

OVERLAPPING RULES, UNIQUE RULES

In this chapter and the previous one, I gathered as exhaustive a list as possible of the rules of each of the four trade regimes at the level that applies to trade in general. Specific international agreements, particularly within the Soviet socialist, mercantilist, or South preferential regimes, will have more detailed rules targeted at certain products or commodities. The rules I have identified here, generally applicable to trade but more specific in nature than norms, order trade on a day to day basis.

Post World War II Liberal, Soviet Socialist, Mercantilist, and South Preferential

The pattern of unique versus overlapping rules gives us insight into how these regimes are distinct yet entwined. First of all, only one rule is held in common by all four regimes: the rule against dumping. But what exactly is dumping? Liberal economists have traditionally defined dumping as "international price discrimination in which an exporting firm sells at a lower price in a foreign market than it charges in other (usually its home-country) markets" (Lindert and Kindleberger, 1982: 164). Recently, however, people espousing views that I have characterized as mercantilist insist that production costs should be calculated to include the under-payment of workers in some countries. Especially when this charge is made by policy makers in industrialized democracies against the labor practices of developing countries and centrally planned economies, the claim points to a belief that foreign firms and governments invade markets and wrest more than their fair share of the market by exploiting workers.

Post World War II Liberal, Soviet Socialist, and South Preferential

Rules against discrimination, for special consideration for developing countries, and for minimum prices for certain commodities can be found in the post World War II liberal, Soviet socialist, and South preferential regimes. Rules against discrimination are fairly consistent across the regimes, although adherents to the South preferential regime would allow "positive" discrimination in favor of developing countries. In the latter two rules, on the other hand, the different regimes interpret the rules differently. Special consideration for developing countries under the post World War II liberal regime include the provisions of the Generalized System of Preferences. Post World War II liberal industrialized countries apply lower tariffs on goods imported from developing countries than from their industrialized competitors, whose goods are imported at the most favored nation rates.

In the Soviet bloc, preferences for developing countries were practiced primarily in within-bloc trade, though preferential arrangements with non-CMEA developing countries may have also existed. The developing CMEA member countries were given protected market shares of certain commodities such as sugar. The special rights for developing countries included in the South preferential trade regime, on the other hand, makes the liberal and socialist considerations look trivial. The South preferential trade regime proposes to restructure international trade in order to guarantee access to markets and reasonable market shares for developing countries on a world-wide basis.

Minimum prices for commodities in the post World War II liberal regime are sanctioned only under unusual conditions. The Tokyo Round of the Multilateral Trade Negotiations Agreement on Dairy explicitly allowed countries to establish floor prices for dairy products. The Soviet socialist and South preferential regimes sanction a broader use of minimum prices.

Mercantilist and South Preferential

Overlapping rules between the mercantilist and South preferential trade regimes point to their similar orientation toward market management. Both regimes agree to the use of export quotas (minimum or maximum amounts to be exported) in order to stabilize markets. The key difference is that export quotas under South preferential rules are used to open markets to developing countries and secure supply for them, while export quotas under mercantilist rules often are used to prevent developing countries from entering the market or increasing their market share.

When viewed from a South preferential perspective, the overlap between the mercantilist and South preferential regimes is dangerous. Because the market management procedures are so similar, South preferential arrangements can be coopted into mercantilist arrangements fairly easily. The difference in intention of the two regimes, however, remains: South preferential market management's goal is to redress unfair distribution of access to markets, while mercantilist market regulation seeks to maintain or restore market hierarchies.

Mercantilist and Soviet Socialist

A similar difference can be found in the mercantilist and Soviet socialist intent of longterm purchase arrangements. The Soviet socialist rationale is to promote stable, state organized growth for the Soviet bloc and developing countries. The mercantilist position favors the protection of sectors of advanced industrialized economies.

Post World War II Liberal and Mercantilist

Rules regarding justifications for safeguarding certain economic sectors appear in post World War II liberal and mercantilist trade regimes. In the post World War II liberal trade regime, policy makers may invoke safeguards only for a limited time during which there is an economic "emergency" for that sector. The protectionist policies employed for this purpose most be imposed without discriminating against certain countries. The mercantilist trade regime, however, sanctions the discriminatory use of protectionist safeguards of economic sectors for unlimited time periods.

Post World War II Liberal and Soviet Socialist

The two dominant regimes of the post World War II period, post World War II liberal and Soviet socialist, agreed on rules prohibiting export licensing to restrain trade, subsidization of exports, and quantitative restrictions on exports and imports. However, the centrally planned nature of Soviet socialist bloc economies render judgements on compliance very difficult.

Unique Rules

The rules that are unique to a single regime further demonstrate the distinctiveness of these trade regimes. The post World War II liberal trade regime, because it is the most formalized and generally accepted, has the most unique rules. Eight of its rules are not shared by the other regimes. Aside from the precise rules of international agreements such as long term purchase arrangements, commodity agreements, and orderly marketing arrangements not catalogued here, the Soviet socialist regime contained four unique rules, the South preferential regime contains two unique rules, and the mercantilist regime contains one unique rule.

That some rules overlap suggests why so much trade is cooperative. That the precise meaning of overlapping rules often differs and that several rules are unique suggests that some trade disputes will concern these issues. That regimes are dynamic social institutions in which the participants argue about creating new rules, changing old ones, expanding the scope, and contracting the scope suggests other forms for trade disputes. That sometimes policy makers choose not to comply with the rules suggests yet another pattern for trade disputes.

* * *

Together Chapters 2 and 3 have systematically examined the content of the post World War II liberal, Soviet socialist, mercantilist, and South preferential trade regimes. The post World War II liberal and Soviet socialist trade regimes have been well established in the international economic system. Today, the dissolution of the Soviet Union resulted in the demise of the Soviet socialist regime. Post World War II liberal trade faces challenges from mercantilist pressures within the industrialized and newly industrialized market economy countries. Pressure on the industrialized world to restructure and create a South preferential New International Economic Order seems to be waning.

All four regimes as described here, I have argued, have had an effect on the way trade is conducted. They have provided the referents that make trade cooperative or conflictual. They provide the structures in which policy makers engage in international trade politics. Regimes are normative; and their principles, norms, rules, decision-making procedures, formal institutions, and codifications provide policy makers with a model for how trade ought to be conducted.

Both the post World War II liberal and mercantilist trade regimes share the principle of the primacy of sovereignty. Both the mercantilist and the South preferential regimes embody notions of stability, although the intent of the stability differs greatly. The special trade rights for developing countries that provide the core of the South preferential regime are contained, in somewhat altered form, in the Generalized System of Preferences of the post World War II liberal trade regime. Discrimination plays an overt role among the mercantilist trade regime adherents and a more subtle role (evidenced by trade flows) in the Soviet socialist bloc. The procedures used by all four orders include negotiations, although the specific form differs.

Despite similarities and overlapping sets of participants, the regimes are distinct. Their underlying ideologies differ; therefore their behavioral prescriptions differ. The institutions and codifications are not the same, nor are the bulk of their principles, norms, rules, and procedures.

The tables that conclude this chapter summarize the elements of the regimes, disputed rules and scope, and overlapping and unique rules. The case study of the sugar trade dispute in the next chapter illustrates how these regime elements frame conflict.

NOTES

1. Interview, 18 November 1992.
2. Interview, 25 November 1992.
3. Contrast my approach to the overall strength of a regime to Haggard and Simmons (1987), who define strength solely in terms of compliance.
4. I have resisted naming this regime "managed trade" because both the mercantilist and South preferential trading regimes embody market management, even though they are grounded in divergent ideologies and principles.
5. Perhaps the GATT secretariat is no different. My myopia with respect to possible lobbying by GATT officials may be simply the result of my socialization to liberal norms.

Table 3-1. Regimes for International Trade

Regime	Principles	Norms	Procedures	Codifications
Post WWII Liberal	Efficiency	MFN GSP	Formal dispute conciliation	GATT
	Sovereignty	Reciprocity Safeguards	Also, bi- and multilateral negotiations	
Soviet Socialist (Soviet perspective)	Anti-Imperialism	State trading	Bi- and multilateral negotiations CMEA discussions?	LTAs Soviet Constitution UNCTAD '79 Conference documents
		* * *		
Soviet Socialist (Western perspective)	Anti-Imperialism Soviet hegemony	State trading Guaranteed supplies to Soviets	Limited negotiations Imposition of Soviet policies	LTAs Soviet Constitution
Mercan-tilist	Market stability Hierarchy ("is/was")	Market regulation Protection of trade rights, market shares	Bi- and multilateral discussions	VERs OMAs Lomé Protectionism
South preferential	Price stability Equity ("ought")	Market regulation Redistri-bution of resources	Multilateral discussions	UNCTAD IPC

Table 3-2. Disagreements among Adherents about the Regimes

Regime	Disputed Rules and Scope	
	Regime Rules	Regime Scope
Post WWII liberal	GSP tariff bindings	all traded items, including agricultural, excluding security
Soviet Socialist —Soviet view	NO ELEMENTS	NO ELEMENTS
Soviet Socialist —Western view	prices payment quality extra-CMEA trade LTA formulation	oil arms machinery and other items
Mercantilist	how and when to protect sectors	commodities and products of threatened sectors
South preferential	formulation and implementation of preferences	commodities and products deemed essential

Table 3-3. A Summary of Trade Rules According to Regime

UNIQUE RULES

National treatment
Reciprocity
Balance of payments corrections
Uniform valuation
Discrimination for national
   security only   Post World War II Liberal
Limits on import licensing   Trade Regime
Limits on technical
   standards
Limits on state trading

Controls on Monopolies
Controls on Capitalist states
State ownership   Soviet Socialist Trade Regime
State monopoly on trading

Discrimination   Mercantilist Trade Regime

Import quotas   South Preferential
Buffer stocks   Trade Regime

OVERLAPPING RULES

Limits on export licensing   Post World War II Liberal
No subsidies   and Soviet Socialist Trade
No quotas   Regimes

Protection of certain sectors   Post World War II Liberal and
                                     Mercantilist Trade Regimes

Longterm purchase   Soviet Socialist and
   arrangements   Mercantilist Trade Regimes

Export quotas   Mercantilist and South
                                     Preferential Trade Regimes

Special rights for LDCs   Post World War II Liberal,
Non-discrimination   Soviet Socialist, and
Minimum prices   South Preferential
                                     Trade Regimes

No dumping   All Four Trade Regimes

Chapter 4

Sugar Trade: Contention Over Rules

"Sugar," write Albert and Graves, "had always been the most political of products" (1988: 3). As a result, the politics surrounding sugar trade are most illustrative of contending trade regimes because the rhetoric of politicking reveals beliefs about rules. That sugar can be produced from both sugar beet and sugar cane heightens the political salience of international sugar markets: Sugar beet grows in the temperate climates of industrialized countries, while sugar cane grows in the tropical climates of many developing countries. Industrialized countries, which have traditionally protected their sugar producing industries, are therefore in direct competition with developing countries. Moreover, instability in international sugar markets has almost always been an expected, though unwelcome, fact of life for sugar producers and consumers. For this reason, trade in sugar has received a great deal of attention both from policy makers and from those analyzing policies.[1]

The story of the politics of sugar trade reveals the different normative claims made by policy makers. The claims, in turn, can be linked to their regimes. In this chapter, I use the dispute over sugar trade to show how the four regimes outlined in the previous chapters — post World War II liberal , Soviet socialist, mercantilist, and South preferential—frame the arguments that surround sugar. My goal is to demonstrate how regimes matter: How they matter to the participants and how they matter in terms of trade practice. *The dispute over sugar trade furnishes examples of how regimes provide the context of trade disputes by filtering the perceptions and interpretations of the participants.* The chapter begins with a discussion of the background of sugar trade and then focuses on the period from 1978 to 1984.

Negotiations on a new International Sugar Agreement began in 1978, culminating in the signing of the 1984 International Sugar Agreement. The negotiations focused a good deal of debate on what the rules of sugar trade should be (Dillon, 1984; Finlayson and Zacher, 1988). I discuss how each regime mattered during this period by analyzing both the words and deeds of the participants. Contrary to common analytical practice (e.g., Odell, 1985), I view this trade dispute as multilateral rather than bilateral since all the different problems concerning this one commodity are very closely interwoven. By using a multilateral focus, I consciously reject a liberal or mercantile view of trade as a bilateral transaction for a view that is more synoptic: Trade, trade cooperation, and trade disputes can be among two or more participants. While a multilateral view is consistent with Soviet socialist and South preferential understandings of international interaction over trade, it can still incorporate liberal and mercantile expectations.

BACKGROUND

There have been many unilateral and multilateral attempts to regulate trade in this commodity since the 1920s.[2] Historically, a relatively small percentage of sugar—about 25 percent in the late 1920s, declining to 10 percent in the late 1940s—was traded freely. The remainder was traded according to preferential arrangements or protected quotas (Albert and Graves, 1988: 7). The United States, the world's largest consumer of sugar, accorded preferential tariffs and guaranteed quotas for sugar imported from Hawaii (before it became a state), the Philippines, and Cuba (before its Communist revolution). Britain, another major sugar consumer, did the same with sugar exported by the countries of the Commonwealth. Currently, only twelve percent of the world sugar market is traded freely, according to Finlayson and Zacher (1988: 123).

Some developing countries are particularly sensitive to instability in sugar markets. Figure 4–1 shows sugar and total exports for the Philippines, the Dominican Republic, Jamaica, and Mauritius, four developing countries that export large quantities of sugar. (Note that the y-axis scales differ on each graph.) Both the Philippines and Jamaica export substantial quantities of sugar, but their economies are diversified enough so that their export earnings are not solely dependent on sugar. Between 1976 and 1986, an average of 8 per cent of Jamaica's total export earnings came from sugar sales. Though that figure fluctuated from 5 percent to 10 percent during the period, there was no evident trend of increasing or decreasing concentration. In the Philippines, the trend was downward, with sugar exports accounting for 17 percent of the total value of exports in 1976 and decreasing to 2 percent in 1986. The decline in sugar earnings during this period was not matched by a decline in total exports.

For the Dominican Republic and Mauritius, however, sugar largely determines export earnings. Both countries' total export earnings are highly dependent on sugar. In all years (except the Dominican Republic in 1977), sugar exports parallel total exports. The Dominican Republic's percentage of total export earnings from sugar varied between 20 and 43 percent, with an average of 30 percent. Mauritius' percentage of export earnings from sugar declined from 75 percent in 1976 to 40 percent in 1986. Despite the decline, 40 percent is a very large proportion of Mauritius export earnings, which would leave the country particularly vulnerable to sugar price fluctuations. For this reason, according to a representative of Mauritius, access of Mauritius' sugar to the EC market, guaranteed support prices at the level that EC farmers receive, and guaranteed purchases of specific quantities are important benefits for the country.[3]

With the exception of Allied controls on sugar prices during World War I, the first formal international accord among producers and consumers was the London International Sugar Agreement of 1937, joined by the United States (which at the time also controlled the Philippines, a major sugar producer), South Africa, Australia, Brazil, Belgium, the United Kingdom, China, Cuba, Czechoslovakia, the Dominican Republic, France, Germany, Haiti, Hungary, India, the Netherlands, Peru, Poland, Portugal, the Soviet Union, and Yugoslavia. To stabilize prices, the Agreement provided export quotas for producers and secured promises of imports from consuming countries. The Agreement never truly functioned because it was suspended when World War II began. After the war, the Agreement was renewed through 1948 (United States Cuban Sugar Council, 1948), though during this period there was no real problem with low prices because of shortages due to the war.[4] Subsequent ISAs were concluded in 1953 and 1958.

Sugar trade came under the aegis of the United Nations in 1965, a year after the UN Commission for Trade and Development (UNCTAD) was founded. A new International Sugar Agreement was not reached until 1968. After the scheduled expiration in 1973, the Agreement was renewed annually to 1977, but without any regulatory activity; the International Sugar Organization functioned only to collect data on sugar trade and act as a forum for negotiating a new agreement. Perhaps as a consequence of the failure to stabilize sugar prices through an international agreement, world sugar prices rose sharply in 1973, and then fell from fifty-seven cents per pound

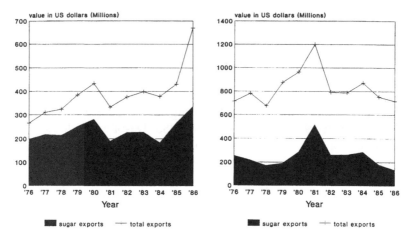

Figure 4-1.1 The Philipinnes   **Figure 4-1.2** Dominican Republic

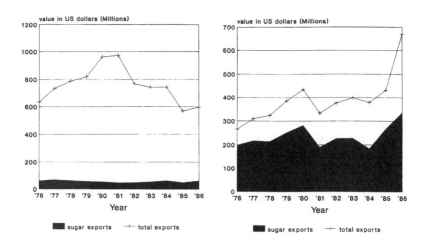

Figure 4-1.3 Jamaica   **Figure 4-1.4** Mauritius

Figure 4-1. Dependence on sugar exports. Source: United Nations *Statistical Yearbook* and *International Trade Statistics Yearbook*

in 1974 to 9 cents per pound in 1978, according to a United States Government Accounting Office report (1979). In 1978, the 1977 International Sugar Agreement went into effect.

Between 1978 and 1984, prices fluctuated severely, though not to the extent that they did before and after this period. In 1984, the 1977 International Sugar Agreement was replaced with a new one. The years 1978 to 1984 represent a period of price instability (see Figure 4-2) coupled with a serious dispute over the regulation of sugar trade. Price instability caused problems for the poorer sugar producing countries, which were unable to plan on a steady income from export earnings. In addition, market shares were an important point of contention. Much of the dispute's substance revolved around whether the EC was exporting an excessively large quantity of sugar and not importing a sufficiently large quantity. Figures 4-3 and 4-4 display the sugar market shares for four main exporters (the EC, Brazil, Argentina, and the US) and imports and exports of sugar, as a percent of world totals, for the EC.

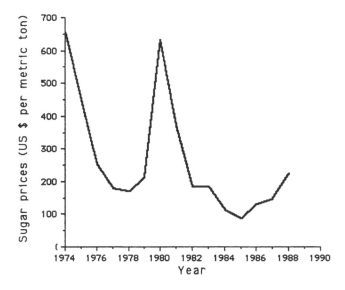

Figure 4-2. World sugar prices. Source: United Nations *International Trade Statistics Yearbook*. Note: The Commodity Research Bureau's *1985 CRB Commodity Year Book* identifies higher prices for 1977 and 1978, based on the spot raw sugar International Sugar Agreement world prices. The pattern of gross fluctuations is, however, approximately the same as reported in the UN publication.

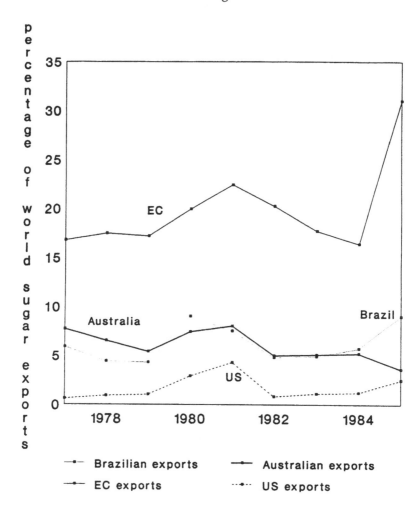

Figure 4-3. Major traders' sugar exports (percent of world markets). Source: United Nations *International Trade Statistics Yearbook*.

Note in Figure 4-3 that in 1977 and 1978 Brazilian and Australian sugar export shares had declined while the EC's share increased. Figure 4-4 suggests that the EC's export market share from 1979 to 1980 was increasing while its import market share was decreasing. These relative changes in the EC's position also exacerbated the dispute. From 1980 to 1983, the EC's percentage of total sugar imports increased while its percentage of total sugar exports

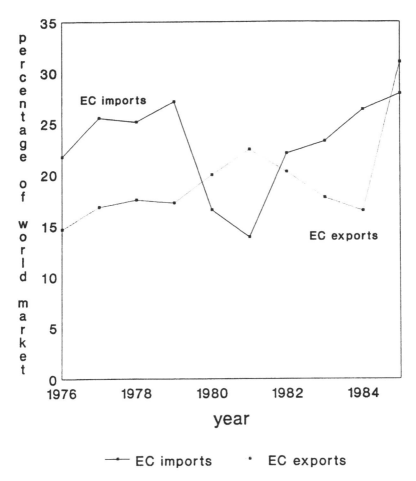

Figure 4-4. EC sugar imports and exports (percent of world market). Source: United Nations *International Trade Statistics Yearbook*

decreased (Figure 4-4). This change, perhaps, helped (after a time lag) to de-escalate the hostilities among the participants in the dispute.[5]

As discussed in the next section, several sugar trade problems were combined in this dispute during this period: the renegotiation of the 1977 International Sugar Agreement, the European Community's continued export of large amounts of sugar at subsidized prices, EC and US sugar import policies, and the Soviet Union's control of its bloc's sugar trade. Information for the synopses of what happened in the politics of sugar trade comes from various issues of *Foreign Agriculture* (a publication of the United States Department of Agriculture), UNCTAD and FAO documents, EC documents, *Foreign Trade* (a publication of the Soviet Union), and data found in the files of the East European Division of the Economic Research Service of the USDA.

REGIME-BASED ACTIONS

A straight chronology of actions taken in the sugar dispute from 1978 to 1984 would miss how regimes framed the dispute. Instead, this section organizes the words and deeds of participants according to the regimes that provide the normative basis for their actions.

Post World War II Liberal Trade Regime Actions

Despite agriculture's special status as an exception to the GATT, several of the participants in the sugar dispute made claims based on post World War II liberal rules. Moreover, participants used the procedures of the GATT to attempt to redress their grievances. The pattern of how the dispute was argued ("fought") shows the problems that GATT members have in convincing other members to play by the rules.

To bring sugar trade into the scope of the GATT, participants questioned whether the EC had violated the GATT's regulations on subsidies. An agreement, adopted during the Tokyo Round in 1979, clarifies the GATT articles on subsidies and provides procedures for an investigation of a country's policies to determine if they conform to GATT rules. The Tokyo Round *Agreement on Interpretation and Application of Articles VI, XVI and XXIII of the General Agreement on Tariffs and Trade* (GATT, *Basic Instruments and Selected Documents*, 26th Supplement, 1980) authorizes an investigation of whether a subsidy is being employed. If so, the GATT is authorized to determine if there has been injury to other countries and whether the subsidy can be shown to be the cause of the injury. If a subsidy is found to cause injury, the affected countries are authorized to impose a countervailing duty. In short, this Agreement prohibits the use of subsidies to give an actor a more than equitable market share.

The European Community's support program for its sugar beet producers allowed the farmers to compete on the world market by subsidizing their exports. According to a 1983 European Parliament report, 54.3 percent of sugar costs in the EC in 1981 came from the cost of export restitution (European Parliament, 1-124/83/B, 10 May 1983). Between 1978 and 1984, members of the GATT deliberated often on the issue of what the EC officially called export refunds to its domestic sugar producers. Bilateral negotiations, invocation of the dispute conciliation process using a panel of economic experts, and multilateral talks all failed to resolve the issue. GATT members that are important sugar producers—Australia, Brazil, Argentina, Colombia, Cuba, the Dominican Republic, India, Nicaragua, Peru, and the Philippines—failed to convince the EC to change its policy despite the rather clear-cut violation by the EC of the Subsidies Code. The EC rejected the GATT determination that its refund program broke the rules embodied in the code and questioned the specific procedures used by the GATT in making the ruling (*Activities of the GATT*, 1978–1984).

In the end the EC's economic strength and the EC countries' claims of sovereignty allowed the EC to ignore the protests of GATT members. Changes in EC policy (shifting the financial burden to the farmers, reducing the amounts of the subsidies) were only in part a reaction to international protests of the policy. The costs of the refund program did more to modify the EC's practice than the GATT did (European Parliament, 1983). Still, the post World War II liberal trade rules codified in the GATT and institutionalized by its procedures provided the setting and the rationale for the playing out of this part of the dispute.

United States sugar import policy was also the focus of a complaint to the GATT. The issue at stake was whether the US should be allowed to keep its waiver of GATT responsibilities in order to continue restrictions on sugar imports (and other agricultural products). Under GATT procedures, the waivers of specific GATT obligations granted to the contracting parties are periodically reviewed. In June 1982, the GATT Council considered the latest annual report from the US on the waiver of US GATT obligations. Other GATT members were not satisfied with the US rationale for maintaining its exemption from the liberal rules.

By November 1983, a working party of GATT members reported that the US had not fulfilled its obligations under GATT and should replace the policies with GATT-consistent ones. The US response to the report was to stress US efforts at curtailing over production of some products and to express that another forum, the GATT

Committee on Trade in Agriculture (as opposed to the GATT Council), would provide the necessary context for liberalization of agriculture, thereby enabling the US to reduce and eliminate the remaining restrictions under the waiver. Members of the working group, particularly Australia, claimed that the US response was an effort at sidestepping the issue by relegating it to a committee. (*Activities of the GATT*, 1982 and 1983). Here the different GATT members again disagreed on the proper procedures to be taken.

As in the case of the European Community, the US did not question the validity of the GATT rule: The US understood that its waiver was temporary and should not be considered a right. The US did question the procedure—the setting for the discussions—and worked within the general framework of the GATT to suggest that discussions ought to be conducted in a specialized committee rather than in the Council. Although the US and the EC may have been pursuing policies inimical to the post World War II liberal trade regime rules, both actors and their adversaries conducted this part of the dispute within the GATT setting. Claims referring to GATT rules were made by all sides. Formalized procedures were used or consciously circumvented. This regime, as represented by the GATT, outlined the rules which the other countries charged the US and the EC were breaking.

Soviet Socialist Trade Regime Actions

Soviet bloc actions included the use of rhetoric to condemn the practices of the EC export subsidies, US import restrictions, and general over production in the developing countries. For example, the Soviet Union blamed the failure of the International Sugar Agreement to regulate prices on the "collusion" (*Foreign Trade*, 6–1978) and "tactical subterfuge" (*Foreign Trade*, 5–1979) of the capitalist countries, as well as "interimperialist confrontation" and recession (*Foreign Trade*, 7–1981). All of this rhetoric focused on the distinction between the Soviet socialist system and the capitalist system. The use of this type of discourse was a common action of representatives of the Soviet socialist regime adherents.

Despite the pro-South rhetoric, the Soviet Union's planned trading within the Soviet bloc and the organization of Cuban sugar exports to other bloc members showed how this regime controlled trade practice as well as rhetoric. According to *Foreign Trade*, advantageous prices for exports of Cuban sugar to the more prosperous Eastern

European bloc members were part of a preferential price system for food trade that would help the poorer bloc members (5–1979). Under the Comprehensive Program of the CMEA to help Mongolia, Cuba, Vietnam, and other countries, Cuba would increase its exports of sugar to the CMEA countries, which would then be able to reduce the area under sugar beet cultivation (*Foreign Trade*, 12–1979). According to USDA documentation, the Soviet Union subsidized Cuba by paying highly inflated sugar prices. Also, while world sugar prices were fluctuating dramatically (see Figure 4–2), the prices the Soviets awarded the Cubans were relatively stable, staying between $809 and $1096 per ton. In contrast, the Soviets paid between $161 and $626 dollars per ton of Brazilian sugar during the same period. It is likely that the Eastern European countries protested these price concessions to Cuba. However, Soviet hegemony probably limited the negotiating power of the Eastern European countries within the institutions of the Soviet socialist regime. Interestingly, Soviet imports of sugar from Nicaragua were not subsidized to the extent that Cuban prices were. In 1987, however, the Soviets paid the Nicaraguans prices marginally higher than world rates for sugar. Traders other than Cuba and Nicaragua received an average of $146 per ton from the Soviets, while Nicaragua received $221 per ton in that year.

Other empirical evidence for Soviet socialist trading can be found in the volume of sugar trade between Cuba and the Soviet Union. Table 4–1 shows percentages of sugar (in quantity) imported by the Soviet Union. Not only did the Soviet Union import most of its sugar from Cuba (although Cuba's market share within the Soviet Union had declined), Cuba consistently exported a substantial percentage of its sugar production to the Soviet Union. This trade pattern of discrimination, with privileges for certain Soviet bloc trading partners, was characteristic of the Soviet socialist trade regime. In addition, the intra-CMEA trade allowed Cuba to circumvent International Sugar Agreement limitations on exports (Smith, 1983: 313–14), thereby increasing the world supply of sugar and contributing to price fluctuations.

Mercantilist Trade Regime Actions

Sugar trade has traditionally been organized on mercantilist principles. Mintz (1985) and Toomich (1990) document the role of

Table 4-1. Soviet Union and Sugar Trade

Year	quantities in thousand metric tons Soviet Sugar Imports			Cuban Sugar Production	
	Total	From Cuba	% From Cuba	Total	% Exported to Soviets
1978	3990	3797	95	7457	51
1979	3778	3707	98	8048	46
1980	3839	2647	63	6787	39
1981	4190	3090	74	7926	39
1982	6161	4224	69	8279	51
1983	4797	2966	62	7250	32

Source: Calculated from USDA, Economic Research Service, Agricultural Trade and Analysis Division, USSR Section, *Database on Soviet Trade.* Project led by K. Zeimetz.

colonialism, the slave trade, and seventeenth and eighteenth century mercantilism in the sugar industry. Attempts in the first half of the twentieth century to control sugar prices often focused more on preserving adequate supplies at low cost to importing countries. Mercantilist tendencies remained during the 1978 to 1984 period.

Although often touted as a major assistance program for developing countries, the Lomé Convention's Sugar Protocol provides, ironically, an example of mercantilist market regulation. The Protocol guarantees that the EC will import certain amounts of sugar from the African, Caribbean, and Pacific countries that are parties to the agreement at supported EC domestic prices. However, this guarantee also serves to manage the market (Mahler, 1981) in a manner injurious to developing countries. Tsadik (1982: 150) points out that quotas for sugar imported by the EC from the ACP countries represent "a serious diminution" of the amounts of raw cane sugar that the ACP states used to supply to Britain. Also, if a sugar exporting country fails, through anything other than *force majeur*, to meet its export quota to the EC, its quota is reduced (Commission of the European Communities, Directorate-General for Information, February 1983, X/64/83). ACP countries are particularly vulnerable because there is no guarantee that the Sugar Protocol will endure. Smith (1981) suggests that the EC imports of ACP sugar will last only as long as Great Britain can provide a market for it.

DiLorenzo, et al. (1983) make a strong argument that even the ostensibly beneficial aspects of the Lomé Sugar Protocol increase the dependence of the ACP countries. Eventually, the authors argue, the "extra" profits generated by sugar sales to the EC at above world market prices will encourage increased sugar production. The ACP countries will then become even more dependent on this single commodity for their export earnings. This outcome is exactly opposite the kind of diversification needed for sustained and stable economic growth.

This Catch 22—aid comes at the price of increased dependence—is typified by the experience of Mauritius. A representative of that country spoke in very positive terms about the Sugar Protocol and the role that it has played in his country. He emphasized that almost all of Mauritius' sugar export is sent to Europe under the terms of the Sugar Protocol, and Mauritius has the largest quota under the Protocol. Mauritius relies on the permanence of the agreement, especially since in 1975 the country's first prime minister decided that it would be better to sell sugar to the EC through provisions of the Sugar Protocol than sell on the world market. The official noted that the Sugar Protocol signifies the long term commitment of the EC to purchase sugar from Mauritius. This guarantee, in turn, has been particularly important because of the central role that sugar plays in the culture and economy of Mauritius. In fact, Mauritius' development plan involves "diversification within sugar," meaning reducing the land under cultivation by one percent per year without a cut in the quantities produced.[6]

Yet even while the representative of Mauritius stressed the benefits of the Protocol, other comments he made (in my view) showed how the agreement increased the dependency of Mauritius on the EC and its largesse. For example, he noted that Mauritius receives the same price for its sugar that EC farmers do, but Mauritius must pay more in freight charges to transport the sugar to Europe. Requests from Mauritius to negotiate the guaranteed price because of the higher freight costs have been denied. Also, while the official was optimistic about the permanence of the agreement, he added that "most say that sooner or later the Protocol will have to be dismantled." And recent and future expansion of the EC may have an overall deleterious effect on Mauritius and other sugar exporters. The representative noted that Portugal had been a sugar importer with a refinery before it joined the EC. With the enlargement of the EC, he said that it had been hoped that the EC would increase sugar import quotas for states exporting under the Sugar Protocol. Instead, the EC has tried to restructure the Portugese sugar refining industry to process beet sugar, produced in Europe, rather than cane sugar, produced in the African, Caribbean and Pacific countries that are member of the Protocol.[7]

Another important point for understanding the role of the mercantile trade regime is that the EC has used its participation in and responsibilities for the Lomé Convention to avoid (until 20 December 1984) signing the International Sugar Agreement. The ISA would have prohibited the EC from continuing its exports of subsidized sugar. The implementation of the Lomé Sugar Protocol without accession to the International Sugar Agreement allowed the EC to maintain its market dominance.

But the EC is not the only actor participating in this agreement. Its ACP partners—the very states which should be least willing to uphold traditional market share rights—are also acting according to mercantilist rules. If the Lomé Convention Sugar Protocol is structured to protect the *status quo* of international sugar trade and the EC's predominance in it, why have the developing ACP countries agreed to it? Why does an official, representing the views of Mauritius, speak so highly of it? The answer lies in the continuation of power hierarchies in the market and the relatively powerless situation of the developing sugar-producing countries. Simply put, the Sugar Protocol is better than nothing. The Protocol is the outcome of bargaining between the ACP and the EC, both of which represented the aggregated interests of their constituent members. The developing countries receive some guarantee of EC purchases, and the EC receives the acquiescence of the ACP partners in the EC's control of the market.

Nevertheless, the bargaining outcome is not targeted at improving the lot of ACP sugar exporting countries. Figure 4–5 below shows EC and selected ACP countries' production and exports of sugar. Between 1980 and 1981, EC sugar production increased sharply. ACP sugar production remained about the same. EC imports of sugar also remained fairly constant. However, ACP exports to the rest of the world declined, reflecting the EC's increased share of world sugar markets. (Refer to Figure 4–4.) Between 1980 and 1981, EC sugar exports increased by 932 thousand metric tons while total sugar exports of those ACP countries examined decreased by 333 thousand metric tons. In effect, EC sugar exports increased in that year at the expense of the ACP and other sugar exporting countries.

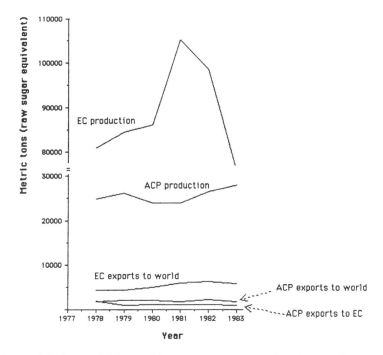

Figure 4-5. Sugar: ACP and EC exports and production. Source: European Community *Analytical Tables of Foreign Trade, NIMEXE*; Food and Agriculture Organization *FAO Trade Yearbook*. Note: ACP countries included in this figure's data are Barbados, Belize, Congo, Fiji, Guyana, Jamaica, Malawi, Mauritius, Trinidad and Tobago, Uganda, and Zimbabwe.

Although opportunism of this scale only happened once during the time period of this study, the outcome is consistent with mercantilist rules. Toward the end of the period studied here, decreased EC sugar production and moderately decreased EC sugar exports, along with fairly constant EC quotas for imports from the ACP countries after 1981, suggest both recognition of resource limitations (the EC program of sugar refunds was too expensive given EC resources) and the continuation of negotiated management.

The United States' Caribbean Basin Initiative (CBI) raises similar issues of intent and effect. The provisions of the CBI included duty-free entry into the US for Caribbean Community products, investment tax credits for US companies interested in investing in the Caribbean, and grants to alleviate the balance of payments problems of these countries. None of these provisions are as beneficial as it appears. Duty-free entry for the majority of Caribbean products was already guaranteed under the Generalized System of Preferences. For the remaining products, many goods, such as textiles, clothing, and footwear, would continue to be subject to US protection. Moreover, sugar import quotas imposed along with the CBI often meant a total decrease in sugar exports from Caribbean countries to the US. Gerard Alexander (1986) states that the Dominican Republic suffered a cut in its sugar quota "from nearly 800,000 metric tons in the early 1980s to some 300,000 tons" in 1986. By appearing to provide a host of benefits to the participants in the CBI, the United States was able to pursue the political goal of maintaining and expanding US influence in the region. This, of course, was at a time when El Salvador and Grenada were high on the public agenda. The US was able to use promises of benefits to restrain (but not eliminate) negative reaction to sugar quotas and then to restrain the negative reaction to the reduction of sugar quotas. The Caribbean Basin Initiative is another example of how a powerful government can carefully balance the pressures of domestic and international interests in creating a market that is less hospitable to developing countries.

South Preferential Trade Regime Actions

The strong normative statements of the call for a New International Economic order were particularly applicable to sugar trade. For adherents to the South preferential trade regime, the purpose of a new ISA would be to find an acceptable redistribution of trade rights and duties to provide a more just market structure. Creating an international, multilateral mechanism such as a commodity agreement for regulating trade is typical of South preferential procedures. The developing country advocates of this regime sought and received the support of international organizations (UNCTAD and FAO) in pursuing a multilateral agreement to regulate the market. Within the International Sugar Organization (ISO), the discussions centered around *how* trade in sugar should be organized rather than whether it should be organized.

Reports released by the UNCTAD and FAO secretariats accused both the United States and the European Community of implementing sugar trade policies which harmed the developing countries. A 1978 FAO Report charged that unstable prices for sugar harmed producers. According to the report, national policies of the more economically powerful countries were protectionist and caused barriers to entry. Especially harmful were the subsidies used to dispose of surpluses on the world market. These general charges were then linked specifically to sugar trade by claiming that the problems faced by the 1978 ISA were that the EC did not join and that the ratification process in the United States was going slowly (FAO, *State of Food and Agriculture*, 1978). These complaints were echoed in later FAO and UNCTAD secretariat reports.

Despite the support of these international organizations, however, the 1977 ISA was unable to regulate the market successfully. Bolivia and Thailand both breached their sugar export quotas during the operation of the 1977 Agreement. In the Thai case, the dispute conciliation procedure was invoked and a panel established to consider the problem. The Bolivian case was resolved in executive committee session. The organization was reluctant to impose the most severe sanctions. Thailand, which exceeded its export quotas twice, was not disciplined by the organization. The participants' reluctance to enforce the Agreement stemmed from four concerns. First, Thailand claimed that the increased exports were unavoidable. Second, it was evident that the Agreement itself was "not working in terms of stabilizing the price (within the target range)." Third (and closely related to the second point), any decrease in ISO member exports, as would be the case if Thailand were fully disciplined, would simply be replaced in the world market by increased European Community exports. Finally, if Thailand had received the severest sanction—exclusion from the organization—it might have become a de-stabilizing, unmanaged exporter like the EC.[8]

Clearly, the ISA has not established a well functioning, widely applied South preferential regime for sugar trade. The 1984 ISA, the result of the renegotiation, was solely an administrative arrangement. It did not regulate exports or imports. This agreement highlights a major weakness of the South preferential trade regime: its members' inability to coerce more powerful countries to accept more responsibilities.

* * *

The case of international negotiations over sugar trade between 1978 and 1984 highlights the different expectations of what the rules should be. Participants articulated rule claims and took other actions consistent with their preferred regime. In conducting this trade dispute, the policy makers of states, international organizations, and private entities made their regime-based understanding of the world

Table 4-2. Summary of pertinent regime characteristics and regime-based actions

Character-istics and Actions	Post World War II liberal	Soviet socialist	Mercantilist	South preferential
Principles	Efficiency; Sovereignty	Rejection of capitalism; maintenance of Soviet domination	Sovereignty; stability; maintenance of hierarchy	Redistribu-tive justice; stability and equity
Rules	Limits on the use of subsidies; limits on GATT waivers	State monopoly on trade; discrimina-tion in favor of Soviet bloc countries	Discrimination in favor of powerful countries	Regulating international markets to create trade rights for developing countries
Institu-tions	GATT	CMEA	Multilateral and bilateral bargaining over Lomé Sugar Protocol and CBI sugar quotas	Multilateral negotiations over the International Sugar Agreement
Codifica-tions	GATT	Various agree-ments regarding sugar trade among CMEA countries	Lomé Sugar Protocol and CBI sugar quotas	International Sugar Agreements
Actions	GATT-centered discussions using new clarification of rules on subsidies and using standard review of GATT waiver; GATT dispute conciliation procedures	Rhetoric stating opposition to capitalist modes of trade; differential pricing for Soviet allies' sugar exports; required purchases of Cuban sugar	discussions over Lomé Sugar Protocol and CBI sugar quotas	ISA-centered discussions; ISA dispute conciliation procedures

clear. As this case shows, regimes can frame disputes as well as foster cooperation. Specifying the differences between regimes presents a clearer picture of what actually happens in sugar trade and situates regimes within the world's larger ideological patterns. Table 4–2 summarizes how regimes influenced actions—both by word and by deed—in the conduct of the sugar trade dispute. The next chapter extends this analysis to the other cases of food and feed trade problems between 1978 and 1983.

NOTES

1. Historical treatments of sugar trade include Tomich (1990) and Mintz (1985). Treatments of economic aspects include Valdés and Zietz (1980), who estimate the cost of OECD countries' agricultural protection policies to developing countries. Sugar is among the commodities analyzed. Social considerations of the current situation is the subject of Coote (1987) and Ramsay (1987).
2. See Finlayson and Zacher (1988) for a contemporary overview of the history of international rule-making for sugar trade. A monograph published by the United States Cuban Sugar Council, an organization of Cuban sugar mill owners, presents a detailed chronology of United States policy on sugar imports from Cuba and the Philippines, including unilateral imposition of restrictions and bilateral agreements (1948).
3. Interview 3 November 1992.
4. Finlayson and Zacher do not concur. They state that the war ended the first ISA (1988: 128).
5. The decline in exports was, however, short-lived. The political effects of increased exports after 1984 are beyond the time period of this study.
6. Interview, 3 November 1992.
7. Interview, 3 November 1992.
8. This information was provided by an official of the International Sugar Organization. Telephone interview, 2 November 1988.

Chapter 5

Regimes and Trade Problems: Looking at Cases

The sugar case presents one example of how regimes matter in the conduct of a trade dispute. To what extent and in what way do regimes matter in general to agricultural trade disputes? I address this question in this chapter by testing hypotheses regarding dispute processes: the initiation of a trade dispute, how hostile and how cooperative the participants' behavior is once the dispute breaks out, the success of mediation and negotiation efforts, and the outcome of the dispute.

FINDING INSTANCES OF TRADE PROBLEMS

I tested these hypotheses on data I coded from descriptions of 62 cases of trade problems, 45 of which became actual disputes. I compiled descriptions of the cases, the synopses, by extracting and cross-referencing information in seven sets of documents and publications from 1978 to 1983:

(1) the United States Department of Agriculture publication, *Foreign Agriculture*;

(2) the *Bulletin of the European Communities* and *Green Europe: the Newsletter of the Common Agriculture Policy* plus information from the files of the EC Delegation Library in Washington, DC;

(3) *Activities of the GATT*;

(4) *Official Records* of the Trade and Development Board of UNCTAD, as well as the *Proceedings of UNCTAD*;

(5) FAO's *State of Food and Agriculture*;

(6) the Soviet Union's *Foreign Trade*; and

(7) supplemental information on the Soviet bloc from clippings in the US Department of Agriculture, Economic Research Service, Eastern Europe Division files.

Note that these sources report behavior and do not codify rules, except in the case of the Soviet bloc. Ideally I would always use separate sources for compiling information on trade behavior and for extracting principles, norms, and rules. When I use separate sources, I eliminate the risk of tautologically arguing that a state behaves according to rules, which come from its behavior. I was unable to maintain this distinction with Soviet sources because of the lack of open information, even now that revolutionary change has transformed the system. The Soviet periodical, *Foreign Trade*, and a document submitted by Soviet bloc countries to the UN Conference on Trade and Development and published in the 1979 Proceedings are sources of both rules and behavior in this study. There is a theoretical reason why using Soviet sources still allows me to avoid the tautological fallacy. The Soviet writings, in articulating problems, clearly stated the rules of the game that had been violated. These sources related the rule and its infraction back to the ideological contention between communism and capitalism. Because these sources were so explicit in their ideological content and normative assertions, it was possible to separate the articulation of the rule (the codification of the rule) from the articulation of its violation (the substantive information on trade behavior).

The information from the East, the West, and the international organizations represent different perspectives on trade. The US, EC, and GATT sources generally reflect the viewpoint of the North; the UNCTAD and FAO reports from the secretariats generally reflect the viewpoint of the South, while reports of statements made by the representatives of different countries reflect the policies of those countries; and the Soviet source generally reflected the viewpoint of the Soviet bloc. The supplementary source on the Soviet bloc presents an alternate picture of actual CMEA trading practices.

I defined a "case" (or trade problem) as an issue which was discussed in the sources. Operationally, if at least one of the sources reported a particular issue as a problem or potential problem, then it became a case. I limited my sample of cases to issues involving food or feed trade. I excluded non-food agricultural products such as cotton and tobacco, as well as issues involving animals and animal products not to be consumed directly (e.g., dairy cows).

A case can be considered a series of "events" which all deal with a specific issue or problem. An event occurs when one country or other actor does something—e.g., makes a statement, complains, imposes an embargo, agrees to negotiations. (See McClelland and Hoggard, 1969; Azar, 1980; note that my use of event requires an actor, but action need not be directed toward a specific target.) An ideal case synopsis would contain a record of all the events that concerned a particular issue. Gathering such data would be an exceedingly time consuming task. It would require knowing about all the actions taken by states, multinational corporations, international organizations, producer groups, consumer groups, etc. I assume that the seven sets of sources that I cite report the major events concerning all food and feed trade problems. Such an assumption seems reasonable because the sources, with the exception of the Soviet sources, do systematically address agricultural trade. The Soviet sources, including the USDA clipping file, address trade issues, though in a less systematic fashion.

Because this study is limited to the years 1978 to 1983, all the trade problems included were referred to in the information sources during those years. Cases need not have ended during the time period of the study, nor have begun during it. For a case to be included in the data file, however, at least one event in the case must have occurred between 1978 and 1983. For example, during this time period *Foreign Agriculture* refers to the 1973 US embargo of soybean exports, the cause of a US-Japanese dispute. This problem is not included in my data file because no events connected to the case occurred between 1978 and 1983.

There are three types of cases: those centering around the policies of nation-states, those centering around particular commodities or groups of commodities, and those centering around criticisms of other regimes. The cases centering around the policies of nation-states, for example, include the trade problems regarding the EC's subsidization of exports, Nigeria's restrictions on imports due to balance of payments problems, and Japanese restraints on agricultural imports. The cases dealing with particular commodities include the disputes involving international dairy trade, international wheat trade, and Norwegian apple imports. The regime criticism cases involve Soviet and socialist bloc problems regarding inter- and intra-bloc trade. The rhetorical content of the cases in which the Soviet Union complains about the rest of the world tend to encompass complaints against all non-socialist agricultural trade relations. (A similar case is one in which the People's Republic of China complains of the same thing.) One case of a trade problem between members of the Soviet bloc focuses on how agricultural trade is conducted among the Soviet Union and its allies.

The cases overlap and are embedded within each other. I decided to make a particular issue a separate "case" when I saw a unified theme in the rhetorical content of the sources. This is clearly a judgement call. The types of things that led me to make an issue a separate case included an article (or section of a document) in one of the sources that dealt solely with that issue. For example, there are several articles in *Foreign Agriculture* dealing with the problems caused by EC agricultural export subsidies, so the issue of EC subsidies is a case. There are also articles on the problems of sugar trade, so sugar trade becomes a case. In the intersection of these two cases is the more specific problem of EC export subsidies for sugar, which does not constitute a separate case, but which is part of both the EC subsidy and sugar cases.

This approach to identifying cases is quite distinct from others' work. Michael Nicholson (1967) and John Conybeare (1985) both limit their investigations to bilateral tariff wars. John Odell (1985: 265) examines a broader vision of trade conflict. He defines international conflict

> as a sequence of actions in which governments take or threaten to take actions that would cause harm to one or more other states. More precisely, an interstate commercial dispute begins when government B responds with a complaint, a counter-measure, or with resistance to a request or trade action by another government, A, which government B believes harms or would harm its trade or economy. Such a dispute ends either when the governments agree to an explicit settlement of their claims, or when communications referring to this episode cease. The terms of the explicit settlement or, in cases without explicit settlements, the behavior equivalent, can be considered the outcome of the conflict.

Odell then examines US-South Korean trade relations and selected those cases when "the value of trade at stake was more than US$50 million during the year prior to the outcome" (1985: 265). In all of his thirteen cases, the identifying characteristic of the dispute is the product that is traded.

This approach, while identifying cases that have recognizable boundaries, has some limitations. First of all, there is no place in Odell's data file for cases concerning general United States complaints about Korean trade policies (or vice versa). Second, this definition assumes that trade disputes are dyadic: Country A and Country B argue it out. But in one example that Odell himself gives, that of negotiations over the Multi-Fiber Arrangement, the disagreements necessarily include other countries. Though negotiations on the MFA were arranged bilaterally, the issue as a whole was dealt with in a multilateral framework. Odell assumes that the only participants that count in trade disputes are states. While states may be the dominant actors, international organizations and other non-state actors can play especially interesting—and independent— roles. Odell's operational criterion for including a dispute in his study (the value of trade in the product must be at least $50 million in the year preceding the outcome of the case) is possibly necessary for limiting the scope of his study. However, the criterion introduces a particularly apolitical capriciousness. A product is as important to the trade policies of a country as the government of the country says it is. If a small, but influential, group of producers is able to raise its product to the national agenda, a trade dispute may ensue. The monetary value of the product is irrelevant, especially since $50 million, or any other arbitrary cut off, means a good deal more to a small country than to a large one.

My approach, in which I read the complaints and identify problems from the substance of the complaint rather than by looking for a particular product at issue, is more representative of differing definitions of problems. In some cases a country may complain about another country's policies for a particular product: The US complaints over Japan's restrictions on beef and citrus imports fall into this category. In other cases, the complaint may be more general: the US demand for negotiations of Japanese structural impediments to trade (the Japanese system of high savings, protection of domestic industries, the retail distribution system, etc.). In yet other cases, the complaint may be more general still: Soviet complaints about the entire capitalist trading system.

While I readily admit the subjectivity with which I have constructed cases of trade problems, I believe that my approach comes closer to letting the participants in the disputes define the disputes' boundaries. This step is crucial in seeing the role that different regimes play in trade because regimes affect how the participants make those definitions.

Who Says What?

The different sources, when put together, offer a richer picture of a dispute than any single source. Looking back at the example of the sugar case, each source had a different focus on what exactly the problem was. The sources and the context of the information provide a partial answer to how regimes are associated with problem recognition. The sources reflect the societies from which they come. Those who write the articles, like all members of the society, see the world through the filters of the societies' dominant regime. Since the sources are all official publications, they reflect the preferred rules of the policymakers of the organization (the US, EC, Soviet Union, UNCTAD or FAO). The case study of sugar trade, discussed in the previous chapter, reveals how different sources frame the problem differently.

Foreign Agriculture, the US publication, reported on the problems of EC export subsidies and on Soviet support for the Cuban economy by purchasing sugar at inflated prices. In the latter case, the trade issue was linked closely to US security concerns about the strength of Castro's regime. EC documents, on the other hand, reported on the internal costs of the export subsidy problem and asserted that the Lomé Convention Sugar Protocol offset any negative outcome for developing countries from EC sugar export subsidies. *Foreign Trade*, the Soviet publication, defined the problem in terms of macro level global capitalist relations, including collusion among capitalist countries, interimperialist confrontation, and the worldwide recession. Though the US and the EC, according to the Soviet publication, were most at fault, the International Sugar Organization also shared part of the blame.

Activities of the GATT reported on the bilateral and multilateral negotiations over EC export refunds and on multilateral disagreement over the continuation of the US waiver that exempts sugar from GATT rules. FAO and UNCTAD documents framed the problems in terms of EC and US actions, suggesting that these countries' reluctance to accede to the International Sugar Agreement, along with their subidies' contribution to price instability, harmed developing countries. Inherently unstable sugar prices were also part of the problem. Table 5–1 summarizes the way each source defines the problems of sugar trade.[1] Ideally, a case synopsis would contain information from each participant. Getting that kind of data on every case is impossible since I want to look at a broad cross-section of agricultural trade disputes. Compiling these different sources is a way of including as many viewpoints as plausible.

Appendix 1 contains more information on how I coded the variables from the case synopses compiled from these divergent sources. This appendix includes operationalizations of the variables. Appendix 2 contains a summary of the description of the distribution of the variables.

Table 5-1. Sources and Problem Definitions in the Sugar Trade Dispute

Source	Definition of problem
US (*Foreign Agriculture*)	EC export refunds. Soviet subsidization of the Cuban economy through inflated sugar prices.
EC various documents	Internal costs to EC for export subsidies. Lomé convention offsets negative impact of export subsidies on developing countries.
Soviet Union (*Foreign Trade*)	Capitalist countries' collusion, interimperialist confrontation, and the global recession. EC and US policies. Unrealistic ISA quotas.
GATT (*Activities of the GATT*)	EC export refunds. US waiver on GATT obligations for sugar.
UNCTAD and FAO various documents	EC and US policies harming developing countries. EC and US reluctance to join ISA. Unstable sugar prices.

DATA ANALYSIS

The central hypothesis of this work, as developed in Chapter 1, suggests that regimes, in conjunction with the economic and political variables, help determine the patterns of trade disputes in the food and feed sector. In Chapter 1, I outlined several more specific propositions that followed from the central hypothesis. Appendix 1 contains information on variable definitions and my coding. Here, I statistically test the following hypotheses dealing with regimes and disputing behavior (initiation of a dispute, actions taken during a dispute, management and dispute conciliation, and dispute outcomes):

Hypothesis 1: Trade disputes are less likely to break out between adherents to the same regime.
Hypothesis 2: Disputes are likely to be less hostile and more cooperative within a regime than across regimes.

Summary of Variables

Dependent variables:
- Initiation of a trade dispute
- Dispute outcome
- Level of hostility
- Level of cooperation
- Success of mediation
- Success of negotiation

Main independent variables:
- Regime adherence
- Pertinence of regime issues

Other independent variables:
- Relative political strength
- Relative economic strength
- Overall level of friendliness
- Importance of agriculture
- Number of participants
- Institutions

Hypothesis 3: The international political system is ill-equipped for undertaking the kinds of dispute conciliation necessary for resolving trade disputes.

Hypothesis 4: The outcomes of trade disputes are more likely to be charaterized by no losers and the satisfaction of all parties in cases involving adherents to the same regime.

I am primarily concerned with the effects of regimes. What tends to happen when the participants adhere to the same regime? To different regimes? And, does it matter whether regime issues are particularly pertinent to the case? Regimes issues are pertinent when the trade problem focuses on what the rules are and how they should be applied. When coding this variable I judged the importance of trade regime issues to the substance of the problem. (See Appendix 1 for more information.) Depending on the hypothesis and its theoretical underpinning, I include some or all of the following macro level independent variables that, I hypothesize, could affect outcomes: the relative political and economic strength of the participants, their overall level of friendliness, the importance of agriculture to the participants' economies, the number of participants, and the existence of institutions for dispute conciliation.

Hypothesis 1: Trade Disputes are Less Likely to Break Out Between Adherents to the Same Regime.

The general understanding is that regimes facilitate cooperation, so I expect that cases are more likely to become actual disputes when more than one regime is involved. When the participants adhere to different regimes, there is more room for disagreement about how traders should behave. This expectation is consistent with previous research in regimes theory that suggests that regimes explain cooperation and lower levels of conflict among otherwise competitive states and other actors.

Alternatively, agreement over the regime may sharpen the understanding of what rules have been broken, so dispute initiation may be more likely when the participants belong to the same regime. For example, GATT-violating policies implemented by GATT members may be more likely to elicit dispute initiation by the affected trade partners that also adhere to this regime. Regime may provide the context in which the rules are better defined and policy makers can more easily identify violations.

The pertinence of trade regime issues to the substance of the case is likely to be associated with dispute initiation. In this case, contrary to the usual theoretical understanding of regimes as promoting cooperation, I expect that trade problems that relate to what the principles, norms, rules, and procedures for trade actually are will be more likely to become disputes than those problems for which trade regimes are not very pertinent to the substance of the case. Trade regimes are not pertinent when policy makers say that the root of the conflict is something other than rules about trade. Instead, the problem might be rooted in security issues, for example.

Asymmetries of power, both economic and political, may have an effect on dispute initiation. Lukes (1974), for example, discusses the role of power differentials in determining whether individuals and groups recognize grievances and act to redress perceived grievances. Bachrach and Baratz (1970) argue that the less powerful will not even be successful at raising their issues to the policy makers' agenda. A similar dynamic is likely to affect trade disputes as well. Less powerful countries may feel that it is futile to initiate a dispute against a powerful trading country. Conversely, more powerful countries may not think it "worth the bother" to initiate a trade dispute against a much weaker actor. Parties of approximately equal strength would be more likely to engage in trade disputes. I test these propositions with reference to asymmetries of both economic and political strength.

One possibility is that trade disputes are less likely among countries and other actors that have a history of amicable relations than among actors which have been contentious toward each other. On the other hand, amicable relations may tend to increase the number of trade interactions, thereby increasing the number of opportunities for disagreements to arise.

Odell (1985) suggests that the probability of initiation of a trade dispute increases as the importance of the sector increases. He argues (and is supported by his analysis of US-South Korean trade disputes) that intra-state interest groups for the more important sectors are more likely to convince their government to initiate a trade dispute than interest groups for less important sectors. I test this hypothesis by looking at the importance of agriculture to the primary plaintiff (side 2).

Finally, as more states and other parties become involved, the issue becomes important to a greater number of individuals. (See Conybeare, 1985.) The issue may also widen in scope. Dispute initiation becomes more likely as more participants see their interests as threatened.

Results. The results of this hypothesis test provide major support for the overall argument of this book: Multiple contending regimes explain cooperation and conflict in trade. The best logit model predicts that trade problems are 8 times less likely to cross the threshold and become disputes when the participants all adhere to the same regime ($p < 0.01$). This finding strongly supports the regimes theory contention that regimes explain cooperation. When participants in trade agree on the rules, they are less likely to conflict. Moreover, this finding points to the importance of identifying issues for which groups of actors advocate different regimes, for it is here that disputes are much more likely to occur. Even though all of the trade problems examined here have to do with food and feed trade—a very narrow issue area—the different normative claims made by the participants about the appropriate set of regime rules has a demonstrable effect on whether problems become disputes.

Adding the other independent variables did not improve the explanatory power of the original logit model because of sparse cells. When I tested the relationships separately, bivariate analyses showed that the pertinence of the regime issues to the substance of the problem, asymmetries of economic strength, and the number of participants were significantly associated with dispute initiation. As expected, the more important regime issues were to the substance of the problem, the more likely it was that a dispute broke out (Goodman and Kruskal's $\tau = 0.28$; $p < 0.01$). Regimes are something of a double-edged sword. On the one hand, adherence to the same regime is associated with a lower probability of a dispute breaking out. On the other hand, disagreements over the regime principles, norms, rules, and procedures are more likely to spark disputes.

Fewer disputes broke out when the economic strength was asymmetrical (Goodman and Kruskal's $\tau = 0.14$; $p < 0.01$). Finally, as Conybeare predicts, the problems that become disputes involve more participants than problems that do not (t with 45 degrees of freedom $= -3.78$; $p < 0.01$). Regimes and the number of participants are probably inter-related: The more participants, the more likely that there will be adherents to more than one trade regime among them. Table 5–2 summarizes the results.

Hypothesis 2: Disputes are Likely to be Less Hostile and More Cooperative Within a Regime Than Across Regimes.

This hypothesis addresses the question of whether regimes can blunt the severity of trade disputes once they have occurred. Ideally, a study of this nature should be able to account for the fine-grained patterns of escalation and de-escalation of hostilities, what has been termed the "phase structure" of disputes. (See Bloomfield and Leiss, 1969; Alker and Sherman, 1982; Farris, et al., 1983; Sherman, 1987.) The studies headed by Bloomfield, Alker, and Sherman, all of which deal with political-military conflict, are rich in detailed information about what happened when. Similarly, events data studies can also focus on subtle changes in the behavior of the participants (e.g., Azar, 1972, 1980; Marlin-Bennett, Rosenblatt, and Wang, 1992). In this mode of analysis, the fluctuations in the intensity of the dispute provide an important key to the conflict dynamics.

Such an approach is not possible within the context of this study because information at the requisite level of detail for these forty-five disputes is not available. Though it is possible to trace the fluctuations in intensity for selected, well-reported food and feed trade disputes, not enough such cases are available for statistical analysis. As a proxy for detailed information on intensity, I examine the extreme actions in a dispute, those of greatest hostility and greatest cooperation.

Table 5-2. Dependent Variable: Dispute Initiaion

Independent Variables	Results	Predicted Direction	Observed Direction
Same or different regimes	Logit model: estimated odds ratio of no dispute initiated to dispute initiated $= 0.88$ for single regime cases, 0.10 for multiple regime cases	Direction not predicted	Almost all cases not within a single regime become disputes
Pertinence of regimes	Goodman and Kruskal's $\tau = 0.28$***	High regime pertinence expected to lead to dispute initiation	Consistent with prediction
Similarity of economic strength	Goodman and Kruskal's $\tau = 0.14$***	Fewer disputes are expected when the participants have dissimilar economic strength	Consistent with prediction
Similarity of political strength	Not significant	Fewer disputes are expected when the participants have dissimilar political strength	Not significant
General friendliness between the participants	Not significant	Direction not predicted	Not significant
Importance of the sector	Not significant	The more important the sector, the more likely a trade dispute would be initiated	Not significant
Number of participants	t with 45 degrees of freedom $= -3.78$***	The more participants, the more likely a trade dispute would be initiated	Consistent with prediction

* $p < 0.1$ ** $p < 0.05$ *** $p < 0.01$

Since regime rules articulate permissible trading and disputing behavior for the participants, agreement over regime rules may moderate behavior in the dispute. When the parties to the dispute adhere to the same regime, the dispute is likely to be less hostile and more cooperative.

The pertinence of regime rules to the substance of dispute should, with the same rationale, have a similar effect. Though regime-oriented problems are more likely to become disputes, they are also more likely to be only mild disputes. My expectation is that disputes involving issues of the regime are likely to be less hostile and more cooperative.

The overall level of friendliness existing between the parties on other issues and the existence of institutions that could act as conflict managers or arbiters are also expected to make the disputes more mild.

Other factors may work against the moderating influence of regimes. For example, the more participants are involved, the greater the opportunity for extreme behavior—more hostile and more cooperative. Extreme behavior would also be associated with the importance of the agricultural sector to the parties. The more crucial agriculture is to a country's economy, the more likely it is to press its opponent as hard as possible. At the same time, the pressure toward conciliation would also be great, especially if the participants perceived that continuing the dispute would be harmful. (Compare Bueno de Mesquita, 1981.)

Results. These data do not reveal the expected relationships. There are two statistically significant associations: The hostility of the dispute is associated with the pertinence of regime issues (Kendall's $\tau_c = 0.32$; $p < 0.01$) and with the general level of friendliness between the parties (Kendall's $\tau_c = 0.17$; $p < 0.10$). In both instances, the direction of the relationship is opposite that which the theory led me to predict. The more amicable the relationship among the parties, the more hostile their food and feed trade disputes are likely to be. The more pertinent regime issues are to the substance of the dispute, the more hostile the dispute is likely to be. This result challenges the view that regimes lead to more cooperative behavior. Instead, regimes may clarify contentious issues, bringing them into the light of day.

Participants' level of cooperative behavior was not statistically significantly associated with any of the explanatory variables. This finding can be explained in different ways. In looking solely at those disputes that occur among the adherents to a single regime, the regime theory expectation is that dispute should be less likely to erupt. Once a dispute does break out, perhaps, the regime no longer functions. Alternatively, how mild the actions of participants are in a dispute may be better explained by variables not accounted for here.

In explaining both extremes of behavior, most hostile and most cooperative actions, the problem of measurement is very important. More interesting than the intensity of the interactions, but much less tractable for formal hypothesis testing, would be how regime rules circumscribe the kinds of actions that are taken in a dispute. Do regimes limit the kind of behavior that constitutes a "fair fight?" Tables 5-3 and 5-4 summarizes these results.

Table 5-3. Dependent Variable: Maximum Level of Hostility

Independent Variables	Results	Predicted Direction	Observed Direction
Same or different regimes	Not significant	Disputes within a single regime are expected to be less hostile	Not significant
Pertinence of regimes	Kendall's $\tau_c = 0.32$***	High regime pertinence is expected to result in less hostile disputes	The higher the pertinence of regime issues, the *more* hostile the dispute
General friendliness between the parties	Kendall's $\tau_c = 0.17$*	The friendlier the participants are, the less hostile the dispute is expected to be	The friendlier the participants, the *more* hostile the dispute
Number of participants	Not significant	The more participants, the more hostile the dispute	Not significant
Importance of agriculture	Not significant	The more important agriculture is to the participants, the more hostile the dispute	Not significant

* $p < 0.1$ ** $p < 0.05$ *** $p < 0.01$

Table 5-4. Dependent Variable: Maximum Level of Cooperation

Independent Variables	Results	Predicted Direction	Observed Direction
Same or different regimes	Not significant	Disputes within a single regime are expected to involve more cooperative behavior	Not significant
Pertinence of regimes	Not significant	High regime pertinence is expected to result in more cooperative behavior in disputes	Not significant
General friendliness between the parties	Not significant	The friendlier the participants are, the more cooperative the behavior in disputes is expected to be	Not significant
Number of participants	Not significant	The more participants, the more cooperative the behavior in the dispute	Not significant
Importance of agriculture	Not significant	The more important agriculture is to the participants, the more cooperative the behavior in the dispute	Not significant

$* \ p < 0.1 \qquad ** \ p < 0.05 \qquad *** \ p < 0.01$

Hypothesis 3: The International Political System is Ill-Equipped for Undertaking the Kinds of Dispute Conciliation Necessary for Resolving Trade Disputes.

Does negotiation or mediation help resolve food and feed trade disputes? Do regimes and institutions make a difference? Formal and informal institutions for the mediation and negotiation of trade disputes exist. The dispute conciliation function of the GATT is a

prime example of a formalized dispute mediation procedure. Meetings of UNCTAD and FAO also have a conflict management
function, though it is less formalized. Conflict management takes
place at these organizations through multilateral negotiations, often
following formal recommendations from the secretariat. Individual
international commodity organizations such as the International
Sugar Organization may also have dispute conciliation procedures
involving third party intervention of some form.

A reasonable inference that can be drawn from the regimes
literature is that regimes are unequivocally cooperative. Consequently, a well-functioning trade regime should incorporate effective
institutions for negotiating and mediating trade disputes. When the
participants belong to the same regime and, therefore, agree on the
appropriate procedures, negotiation and mediation are more likely to
be successful. Similarly, the more the substance of a regime pertains
to regime issues rather than other political or military issues, the
more effective negotiations and mediation should be. In contrast, my
expectation is that regime adherence will not have an effect on the
success of negotiation and mediation and that the pertinence of
regime issues may well decrease the success of negotiation or
mediation. I derive this expectation from my rejection of the purely
cooperative view of regimes.

If regimes have an effect, negotiation and mediation should be
most successful when conducted in the context of institutions in
which all the parties to the dispute have a voice. Producer groups
and multinational corporations, for example, may be active participants in a trade dispute, but no institution now incorporates their
participation in negotiations. Moreover, some of the states involved
in a dispute may not belong to the organization in which the
mediation or negotiation is taking place. This is sometimes the case
with disputes raised before the GATT Council.

Great differences in political and economic power, however, may
outweigh the effects of regimes and institutions. Even if a mediator
suggests a compromise favoring the weaker party, no current regime
provides an enforcement mechanism. In negotiations, the more
powerful side may simply impose a solution.

Results. As expected, institutionalized negotiation and mediation
are not particularly effective ways to resolve food and feed trade
disputes, despite the procedures that are part of regimes. In fact, only
the relationship between the success of negotiations and the
pertinence of regime issues showed a significant relationship (Ken-

Table 5-5. Dependent Variable: Success of Negotiation

Independent Variables	Results	Predicted Direction	Observed Direction
Same or different regimes	Not significant	Predicted no significant relationship	Not significant
Pertinence of regimes	Kendall's $\tau_c = -0.34$*** (very sparse tables)	Negotiation less successful in disputes about issues that are highly pertinent to regimes	Negotiations are less successful in disputes in which regime issues were highly pertinent
Institutions	Not significant	Negotiation more successful when institutions including all the parties to the dispute exist	Not significant
Similarity of economic strength	Not significant	Negotiation less successful when the parties' economic power is asymmetrical	Not significant
Similarity of political strength	Not significant	Negotiation less successful when the parties' economic power is asymmetrical	Not significant

* $p < 0.1$ ** $p < 0.05$ *** $p < 0.01$

dall's $\tau_c = -0.337$; $p < 0.01$), though the sparseness of the contingency table makes statistical interpretations a bit ambitious.

The direction of the relationship is particularly interesting. Looking only at the 37 disputes that involved negotiations, the more pertinent regime issues are to the substance of the case, the less successful negotiations tend to be. Most telling are the simple frequencies for the success of mediation and negotiation. Negotiation, whether bilateral or multilateral, is very successful in only about 16 percent of the food and feed trade disputes I examined. Mediation is very successful in only about 7 percent of the disputes.

These findings substantiate the proposition that the international system lacks effective mechanisms for trade dispute conciliation. Many would argue that the problem is simply one of a single evolving (or dissolving) regime. I argue that multiple, contending regimes explain, in large measure, the failure of the international system to develop effective dispute conciliation. Tables 5-5 and 5-6 summarize the results.

Table 5-6. Dependent Variable: Success of Mediation

Independent Variables	Results	Predicted Direction	Observed Direction
Same or different regimes	Not significant	Predicted no significant relationship	Not significant
Pertinence of regimes	Not significant	Mediation less successful in disputes about issues that are highly pertinent to regimes	Not significant
Institutions	Not significant	Mediation more successful when institutions including all the parties to the dispute exist	Not significant
Similarity of economic strength	Not significant	Mediation less successful when the parties' economic power is asymmetrical	Not significant
Similarity of political strength	Not significant	Mediation less successful when the parties' economic power is asymmetrical	Not significant

* $p < 0.1$ ** $p < 0.05$ *** $p < 0.01$

Hypothesis 4: The Outcomes of Trade Disputes are More Likely to be Characterized by No Losers and the Satisfaction of All Parties in Cases Involving Adherents to the Same Regime.

This hypothesis looks at how trade disputes end. John Burton (1984) points out the difference between resolution and settlement of a conflict. Resolution, he suggests, means that an equitable solution pleasing all participants has been found. Settlement, in contrast, means the imposition of the will of one of the parties on the others, regardless of whether the disadvantaged side has acquiesced or not. Outcomes of trade disputes can also be thought of in this way. Trade disputes could be characterized as "not necessarily zero sum games," in which the outcome depends on which side, if any, won and how satisfied all the participants were. Who won and satisfaction are the two variables that serve as proxies for dispute outcomes.

Regimes may contribute to cooperative dispute endings. Specifically, the theory leads me to expect that disputes among adherents to a single regime are more likely to have a good outcome: no losers and satisfaction of all the parties. Participants adhering to the same regime have similar expectations about proper trading behavior and dispute conciliation. Often they are close allies with similar cultures as well—other signs of similar beliefs. In contrast, the expectation is that good outcomes will be less likely when the participants adhere to different regimes. Their expectations will be more divergent, so it will be more difficult for them to find a mutually satisfactory compromise.

Under certain conditions, though, disputes involving only a single regime may well have a less positive outcome. If, for example, the regime is evolving and new rules are being developed, the participants may not have reached a consensus. The development of the Subsidies Code of the GATT is an example of a new rule that has contributed to poorer outcomes for disputes among GATT members.

The pertinence of regime rules may also enter into the relationship. Positive outcomes, in terms of satisfaction and resolution, are more likely when regime rules are pertinent to the substance of a dispute among adherents to the same regime. Pertinence of regime rules may have an opposite effect on disputes among adherents to different regimes.

While generally good relations may facilitate reaching good outcomes, power may be an important determinant. John Odell's 1985 study of United States-South Korean trade relations partially

supports his hypothesis that the stronger prevail over the weaker in
trade disputes. More economically or politically powerful parties
could simply enforce settlements on their weaker trading partners.
Conversely, some powerful actors may choose not to enforce a
settlement against a weaker participant if the value of the issue is not
important to the stronger party.

The number of participants involved is expected to decrease the
probability of a good outcome simply because the more participants
there are, the less likely all will be satisfied. Finally, disputes among
close allies are more likely to have good outcomes because the
participants would have a history of successful cooperation.

Results. The interpretation of the statistical tests for this hypothesis
is difficult because of the small number of disputes with good
outcomes. Despite the hypothesized relationship, adherence to the
same regime is not associated with better outcomes of trade disputes.
As common sense would suggest, the number of participants in the
trade dispute is strongly associated with the outcome of the dispute:
It is hard to please all the people all the time, and the more people
there are, the harder it is to please them. In all five of the cases that
ended without any side losing, there were only two participants. In
the rest of the disputes, the mean number of participants was about
23 (skewed by several cases involving almost all developing countries) with a good deal of variation. The difference in means between
the two groups was statistically significant (t with 39 degrees of
freedom = 4.05; $p < 0.02$). The results for the satisfaction of all
parties were very similar. The mean number of participants was
about 24 for the group of disputes that did not end with all sides
satisfied; the mean number of participants was about two for those
disputes that did end with all sides satisfied (t with 38 degrees of
freedom = 3.99; $p < 0.02$).

Two independent variables—regime pertinence and the overall
level of friendliness of the parties—seem to be associated with the
outcome of trade disputes as measured by who won and how
satisfied all the participants were. However, there was not enough
variation among the forty-five disputes to claim statistical significance. The apparent direction of the relationships is interesting,
though further research would be needed to confirm it. As the amity
between the participants in a trade dispute increases, the likelihood
of all parties being satisfied and the likelihood of no side losing
decrease. Likewise, the more pertinent regime issues are to the
substance of the dispute, the less likely that all sides will be satisfied

and that no side will lose. This result would be consistent with the associations of these two variables with the levels of hostility. Table 5-7 summarizes the results.

Table 5-7. Dependent Variables: Who Won? And Satisfaction

Independent Variables	Result	Predicted Direction	Observed Direction
Same or different regimes	Not significant	Single regime disputes would have better outcomes	Not significant
Pertinence of regimes	Apparent direction is negative, but sparse tables preclude claims of significance	High regime pertinence expected to result in better outcomes	All the parties are less likely to be satisfied when the pertinence of regime issues is high
General friendliness between the participants	Apparent direction is negative, but sparse tables preclude claims of significance	Generally amicable relations expected to result in better outcomes	All the parties are less likely to be satisfied when the parties are generally friendly toward each other
Similarity of economic power	Not significant	Poorer outcomes expected when one side is stronger	Not significant
Similarity of economic power	Not significant	Poorer outcomes expected when one side is stronger	Not significant
Number of participants	Who won: t with 39 degrees of freedom = 4.05** Satisfaction: t with 38 degrees of freedom = 3.99**	The more participants, the poorer the outcome	Disputes with fewer participants were more likely to have outcomes of no side lost and all sides satisfied

* $p < 0.1$ ** $p < 0.05$ *** $p < 0.01$

* * *

The theory of multiple regimes does best at predicting when trade
disputes will break out. When traders have differing beliefs about
the appropriate rules of the game for trade—when they adhere to
different regimes—trade disputes are much more likely to break out
once problems are recognized. This is a straightforward interpretation, consistent with the usual understanding of regimes as explaining why cooperative behavior is rational in what Realists see as a
competitive world.

But regimes do not have a strictly cooperative role to play. The
pertinence of regime issues to a trade problem is the measure I have
used. Assuming reliable coding, contending rule claims may exacer-
bate conflicts. Paradoxically, regimes may serve to highlight inconsistencies in expectations among trade participants. Negotiations
over what the rules should be may well be contentious, perhaps
more intractable than trade disputes in which the policy makers do
not explicitly make claims about how trade ought to be conducted.

This point is brought home by the failure of regimes to provide
effective dispute conciliation. Though regimes may help to prevent
conflict from arising, once it does arise, regimes do not seem to offer
procedures for resolving the dispute.

The description of the diversity of trade problems and regime rule
claims and the formal hypothesis testing of this chapter lend
credence to the central hypothesis presented in this book. Food and
feed trade is best understood by looking at contending regimes.
Regimes explain both why cooperative trading takes place and what
happens when cooperation breaks down and disputes break out. The
next chapter continues exploring hypotheses about regimes and
trade disputes by looking at patterns of trade problems.

NOTE

1. Though in writing the case study I included information from secondary sources,
   I am limiting this discussion of who said what about sugar to the seven sources that
   I actually used to compile my coded data.

Chapter 6

Order and Disorder in the World of Trade and Trade Disputes: Regime Explanations

Trade problems are not discrete, easily identifiable occurrences in international relations. In fact, no international conflict can exist in isolation. Take, for example, the Arab-Israeli conflict. Is this a single conflict or a series of conflicts? Were the United States and the Soviet Union parties to the conflict? If so, were parts of the Arab-Israeli conflict somehow linked to the Cold War? How about the Lebanese Civil War? Certainly it is related to the Arab-Israeli conflict in some way.

Most classic quantitative studies of international conflict finesse this issue through tidy operational definitions (Singer and Small, 1972; Butterworth and Scranton, 1976). My approach is different. Though I too have had to make operational choices about what constitutes a dispute, I believe that the way in which cases are interconnected contains important information about the similarity and dissimilarity—order and disorder—among cases. Instead of viewing blurred dispute boundaries as a problem, I analyze the way in which those boundaries are blurred.

This chapter focuses on the connections between cases and interprets the role that regimes play in creating those ties. The existence of a single regime would suggest that there should be a pattern to trade problems because a regime suggests rules and orderly behavior. The existence of several contemporaneous regimes should be manifest in a much more complex pattern in the connections between cases: a disorderly system, in fact. To restate the proposition I evaluate in this chapter, *we should recognize the disorder of trade constrained by multiple regimes in the patterns of trade problems and in the way regimes order how cases overlap.* But this disorder still should be distinguishable from anarchy. In fact, regimes allow us to make sense of the disparate problem definitions and rule claims of trade disputes. I look at two kinds of connections between cases.

First, how are trade problems linked by commodity, issue, and actors? The disputes involving sugar trade and cocoa trade, for example, are connected because both involve, in part, discussions over the formation of international commodity agreements. Similarly, cases involving EC barriers to trade, EC export subsidies, and the possible negative trade effects of the expansion of the EC are joined because they all involve the EC. The case involving the negotiations over the International Coffee Agreement connects with the one involving Spain's restrictions on coffee imports because both have to do with coffee. Regimes order these connections because regimes frame problems. How a policy maker perceives a problem, and hence how that policy maker articulates grievance about another or defends her or his country (or firm or group) depends on regime-based ideas about the extent of the problem.

Second, how are trade problems linked by the principles, norms, and rules that these policy makers use to argue their position? For example, all cases that involve a disagreement over whether a government can use trade policy to protect a sector it deems vital share a particular focus. Of these cases, the ones that also involve contending claims about what constitutes a reciprocal reduction of trade barriers are even more closely linked. Regimes, by providing the principles, norms, and rules to which policy makers refer, structure these links.

The extent to which certain combinations of principles, norms, and rules occur more frequently than others shows what is most contentious. Of special interest is whether certain principles, norms, or rules from one regime often occur in combination with certain principles, norms, or rules from another regime. One potential example of this would be the norm of non-discrimination for the post World War II liberal regime and the norm of discrimination for the mercantilist regime. These norms, of course, are opposites. But do adherents of the post World War II liberal and mercantilist regimes reference their respective norms when they engage in trade disputes? If they do so repeatedly, then the different values encoded in these regimes' norms have important implications for policy. This would be an important point at which the two regimes penetrate each other and lead to conflict. If discrimination and non-discrimination do not often appear together as the contested norms in a trade dispute, then the two regimes would be disjoint at that point, suggesting that the contradicting norms of the two regimes have no effect on policy.

CONNECTIONS BY COMMODITIES, ISSUES, AND ACTORS

Regimes order how trade problems are connected by the commodities, issues, and actors. For the adherents of the post World War II liberal regime, trade problems are fundamentally bilateral affairs. Trade is viewed as a contractual arrangement. Contracts are usually bilateral. The structure of the GATT's dispute conciliation process reflects this focus. Moreover, the cases center around the relations between two traders, usually states. A complex problem between two states might be further broken down by commodity at stake.

For adherents of this regime (and for the analysts trained in liberal economic thought), the distinction between disputes becomes tractable. Since the borders of countries are easily identified, the boundaries between disputes are too. A dispute between the United States and Japan over the export of US beef is clearly distinct from a dispute between the United States and the EC over the export of US beef. The only questions are about the connections between the US-Japanese dispute over beef and the US-Japanese dispute over semi-conductors.

The perspective of the Soviet socialist regime depended on the issue. Trade problems concerning non-socialist countries were framed in global terms. Public statements from Soviet sources during the period when those statements were closely scrutinized for ideological correctness stated that "the problem" was the entire capitalist system. Since all the different issues could be traced to a single cause—capitalist trade—all the issues were simply components of a larger problem.

Trade problems within the Soviet bloc (as inferred form the work of Sovietologists and Eastern European specialists from the West) were defined in terms of the East European countries versus the Soviet Union and its authority. While these cases may have dealt with certain products (e.g., oil), the problem was defined in terms of the power inequality and hierarchical nature of intra-bloc relations.

Mercantilist traders define problems by either the product or the countries because they are concerned with maintaining market shares. If Country A's share of the market for a particular good is threatened, the problem may be defined by the product. If, on the other hand, several products from Country B threaten the market

Food Fights

position of Country A, then the problem will be defined as a dispute between A and B. If more than two countries are involved, then the problem will be defined as multilateral rather than bilateral.

In contrast, adherents of the South preferential regime always define problems by the commodity at stake, and all problems are multilateral. This is consistent with the regime's procedure of coordinated action and the institution of commodity agreements. When adherents of this regime press complaints about trade policies, they create a coalition with other South preferential adherents to maximize their political influence. For example, in the case of the dispute over sugar trade, representatives of South preferential participants in the dispute referred to the problem of sugar trade in its entirety. The policies of the European Community and the United States were components of the sugar trade dispute, but the dispute was over sugar trade as a whole and not broken down into an EC-Third World Sugar Producers dispute and a US-Third World Sugar Producers dispute. The creation of commodity agreements reflects this attention to the commodity itself.

In short, trade problems are defined in terms of:

(1) the countries or other participants involved (post World War II liberal and sometimes mercantile definitions),
(2) the issue at stake (Soviet socialist definition), or
(3) the commodity at stake (South preferential and sometimes mercantile definition).

Blurry Boundaries of Disputes

The fuzziness of dispute boundaries comes from the possibility that a problem defined by one of the criteria above (say, for example, the countries involved) pertains to the same commodity as a problem defined by that commodity, another criterion. For example, the dispute over EC export subsidies (a case defined primarily by who the participants are) deals with some of the same complaints and normative claims as the dispute over sugar trade (a case defined primarily by the commodity). In a similar vein, all cases involving commodities are linked because the Integrated Program for the Commodities unites them. Likewise, all cases involving US trade policy are linked because they have to do with the United States.

The connections between disputes can be illustrated by examining the sugar trade dispute. The sugar case overlaps with the cases involving tea, wheat, cocoa, coffee, and bananas because of the issue involved. Each of these cases deals with the negotiation of international commodity agreements. In addition, each of these cases is framed by South preferential concerns of redistributing market shares to those countries that have been placed at a disadvantage by the current system and of providing stable prices.

The issue provides the link between the sugar dispute and other commodity oriented cases. The cases involving trade in oils and the International Meat Agreement are in this category. In both cases, there was an attempt within the Food and Agriculture Organization to create "guidelines" for trade in these products, essentially an alternative to UNCTAD's commodity agreements. This attempt to formulate guidelines, an action consistent with South preferential procedures, links these cases to the sugar trade dispute in which the UN agencies worked to form a commodity agreement. Both of the cases are also framed by mercantile attempts at organizing market shares inequitably and liberal attempts at reducing barriers to trade in these products.

Two cases framed by references to a particular country's (or in the case of the EC, organization's) actions are also related to the sugar case, this time because of the participants. The sugar trade dispute looks at all countries' problems with sugar trade. The EC subsidies dispute and the US import restriction dispute look at all EC subsidized commodities (including sugar) and all commodity imports restricted by the US (including sugar), respectively. The case involving US import policy is framed around mercantilist concerns over the distribution of market shares within the US economy and different industries' attempts to limit import penetration. One of the commodities whose entry into the US is restricted is sugar. A similar dynamic is at play with the case involving EC export subsidies. Sugar is one of the products which the EC subsidizes in a mercantilist attempt to order the distribution of market shares within the EC.

The sugar trade dispute overlaps with the US-Nicaraguan trade dispute because the commodity at stake was sugar: The US restricted imports of sugar from Nicaragua because of US opposition to the Sandinista government. The US-Nicaraguan trade dispute is framed by mercantilist conceptions of hierarchy and dominance.

These cases that overlap the sugar dispute because of similar issues, participants, or commodities also overlap with other cases for these same reasons. Sometimes they overlap with the same cases. Sometimes these "second order" (viewed from the perspective of cases overlapping with the sugar trade case as "first order") overlapping cases overlap with each other. The diagram below is a partial depiction of the connection between cases surrounding the dispute over sugar trade. The complexity of the diagram shows how dispute boundaries can be fuzzy due to similarities between cases.

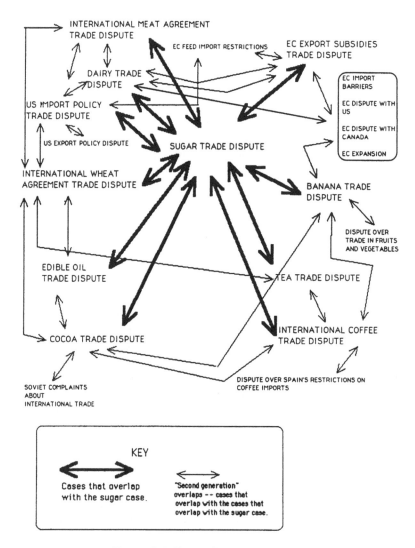

Figure 6-1. Blurry dispute boundaries.

A Generalized Picture of Blurry Boundaries

The next step in this analysis is to look at all the cases to see how they overlap on issue, participants, and commodity. Figure 7-2 is an informal representation of the similarity between cases based on the application of a technique called Multi-Dimensional Scaling. An explanation of this technique and the actual results of its application can be found in the appendix.

Of the 62 cases I examined, only 14 cases do not overlap with any others based on the issues, participants, and commodities.[1] Sixteen cases overlap with one other case, five cases overlap with two others, three cases overlap with three others, four cases overlap with four others, and twenty cases overlap with five or more other cases.

The cases that do not overlap with any other cases can be found on the right side of the circular pattern, or circumplex. They are similar each other because they all have less fuzzy boundaries than the other cases. On the left side of the picture are cases that are more closely interrelated. Several cases involving the European Community's trade policies are represented. Cases that are similar to each other because they all deal with issues involving commodity trade agreements overlap with some of the EC cases and with each other. Among these are the cases overlapping with and including the sugar trade dispute. The commodity cases are located close to the EC cluster. Cases involving the United States as a major participant are more spread out, a visual representation of either the ubiquity of United States trade interests or the American bias of the data.

The cases that do not overlap others represent, in most cases, bilateral disputes between the US and another country. The post World War II liberal assumption of trade as a bilateral contractual arrangement is represented in this way. The problem of identifying a case becomes much more apparent when participants operating under different regime-dependent conceptions of what the problem *is* negotiate with each other. Different problem definitions can lead to representatives talking past each other because they do not have a common idea of what the dispute is all about. The obstacle to resolving disputes is particularly apparent when the representatives are adherents of different regimes.

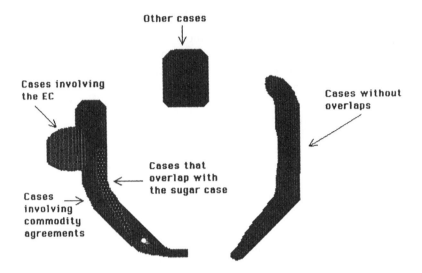

Other cases

Cases involving
the EC

Cases without
overlaps

Cases that
overlap with
the sugar case

Cases
involving
commodity
agreements

Figure 6-2. How cases overlap.

PATTERNED COMBINATIONS OF PRINCIPLES, NORMS, AND RULES

Another way for cases to be tied to each other is by similarities in the claims made by the participants in each case. Policy makers articulate or imply the principles, norms, and rules that provide the rationale for why their side is right in a disagreement. In cases of agricultural trade problems and disputes, very often the policy makers talk past each other in this regard as well: They have completely different rationales for why what they are doing is right and what the other side is doing is wrong. Other times, the policy makers agree on the applicable rule but disagree on its interpretation.

Regimes determine what possible claims a participant can make because regimes contain the principles, norms, and rules for trade. The participants on all sides may agree on the principle, norm, or rule at stake, but they may disagree over its interpretation. Alternatively, the participants may disagree over the principle, norm, or rule that applies. When the participants adhere to different regimes, the opportunities for disagreement over which principle, norm, or rule applies are much more numerous. Table 6-1 summarizes how regimes structure agreement or disagreement over principles, norms, or rules in trade problems.

Table 6-1. Regimes and Agreement and Disagreement on Principles, Norms, or Rules

Agreement or Disagreement on Principle, Norms, or Rules	Interpretation
A and B agree on the applicable principle, norm, or rule.	Participants interpret the principle, norm, or rule differently. (For rules that overlap different regimes, different interpretations may represent differences between the regimes.)
A and B disagree on the applicable principle, norm, or rule, and . . .	
A and B adhere to the same regime.	Vagueness or contradiction within the set of regime principles, norms, and rules.
A and B adhere to different regimes.	Contradictions between the principles, norms, or rules of the regimes.

An Example

The sugar trade and EC export subsidies cases provide an example for showing how principles, norms, and rules relate cases to each other. I coded four sides for the sugar trade case. The primary defendant was the European Community. In defending actions regarding sugar trade, EC officials made reference to the principle of creating stable markets, the norm of protecting trade rights and market shares, and the rule allowing the protection of certain sectors of the economy. All of these claims are consistent with the mercantilist trade regime. The primary plaintiff side was composed of Australia, Brazil, and other developing countries. Their representatives charged that the EC has violated the principle of equity, the norm of market regulation, and the rule requiring import quotas that benefit developing countries. (Under the Sugar Protocol of the Lomé Convention, the EC did have sugar import quotas, but not to the satisfaction of these plaintiffs.) The claims made by this side came from South preferential expectations about proper trade behavior.

Side Three consisted of the United States and a US firm, Great Western Sugar. The representatives of this side, conforming to post World War II liberal regime expectations, charged the EC with overstating the Community's sovereignty regarding economic affairs (a principle) and with failing to honor reciprocal arrangements (both a norm and a rule). The fourth side, the Soviet Union, referred to the Soviet socialist principle of anti-imperialism, the norm of state trading, and the rule requiring the need to place controls on capitalist states.

There are some similarities between the sugar case and the EC subsidies case. The dispute over EC export subsidies was basically bilateral, with the EC as the defendant and the US, Australia, and developing countries as the plaintiffs. The representatives of the EC, when referring to the whole of EC export restitution policy, implied a need to maintain hierarchical market shares (a principle), to protect trade rights and market shares (a norm), and to engage in discrimination (a rule). All of these come from the mercantilist trade regime. The plaintiff side, in contrast, argued that EC export subsidies violated the post World War II liberal principle of efficiency, the norm of most favored nation status (the subsidies meant that MFN was abrogated), and the rule that prohibits countries from using subsidies to get a greater market share than they would have in a free market.

In both of these cases, the EC representatives made claims about its right to protect market shares. This is the point at which these two cases overlap in terms of their principles, norms, and rules. At a level finer than can be revealed in cross-sectional data of the type that I have collected, there is even greater correspondence between the two cases because the principle and rule articulated by EC representatives in the sugar case are also referenced in the EC export subsidy case, though not as strongly as the principle of hierarchy and the rule allowing discrimination. The reverse is also true: Maintaining hierarchy and allowing discrimination are the secondary principle and rule for the EC in the sugar dispute.

Completely different from either of these two cases would be a case like the dispute over intra-Soviet bloc trade. In this case, the Soviet Union was the defendant, and Bulgaria, Romania, and other CMEA countries were the plaintiffs. Both sides agreed on the principle (Soviet hegemony), norm (guaranteed supplies to the Soviets), and rule (state monopoly on trading) at stake. However, the Soviet Union argued that this combination of principle, norm, and rule was appropriate and should be a part of the regime, while the other CMEA countries argued that the principle, norm, and rule were unfair.

Figure 6-3 portrays how the principles, norms, and rules of these three cases do or do not overlap.

Looking at More Cases

The next step in this analysis is to look at the similarities and differences in the cases' principles, norms, and rules, which I coded by interpreting published documentary accounts of the case. (See Appendix 1 for more information on coding.) If there were only one regime, I would expect to find that there would be little variation in the combination of principles, norms, and rules. This would be true

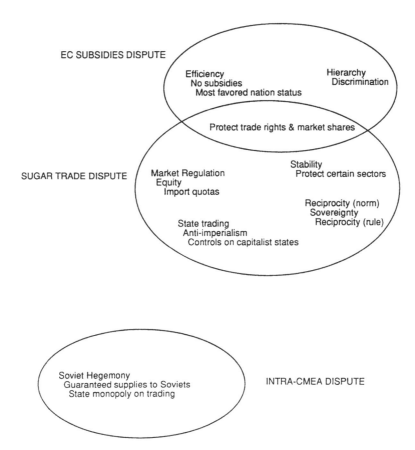

Figure 6-3. How the principles, norms, and rules of cases overlap.

for two reasons. First there would be few principles, norms, and rules; and second, an even smaller number of these principles, norms, and rules would likely be contested. In other words, the picture that mapped the similarity of cases on the contested principles, norms, and rules should look much like Figure 1-1.1, a Venn diagram that depicts the usual definition of a regime. This figure is reprinted as Figure 6-4 below. If there were multiple regimes but no trade among adherents to different regimes, the sets would be disjoint. Figure 6-5, reprinted from Figure 1-1.3, shows that relationship.

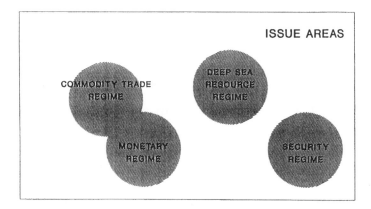

Figure 6-4. Usual definition.

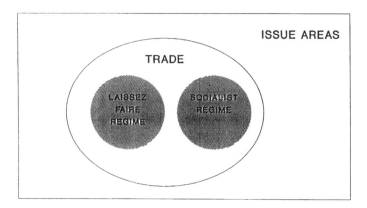

Figure 6-5. Young's definition.

Instead, I expect to find—and do find— a much more complex picture, one which is consistent with the way different participants in trade disputes may invoke different principles, norms, and rules and may adhere to different regimes. The picture I expect to see would be consistent with the Venn diagram that depicts a multiple regime framework (Figure 1-1.4, reprinted as Figure 6-6 below). Because trade takes place among adherents to different regimes, the clusters of cases should intersect.

To look at the similarities and differences among the combinations of principles, norms, and rules in all 62 cases I examined, I again employed the technique of Multi-Dimensional Scaling. The figures below are representations drawn from that analysis, while the actual results of the analysis are found in the appendix.

Patterns of principles. The clusters of disputes shown in Figure 6-7 represent, primarily, a division between East and West—between Soviet socialist and post World War II liberal principles. Cases involving mercantilist and South preferential principles overlay the whole. Common combinations of principles emerge in the diagram. Ten cases, for example, all involve contending views of sovereignty. Two cases involve only disagreements over what constitutes efficient policy. In fourteen cases, one side articulated its argument in terms of sovereignty while the other side articulated its argument in terms of efficiency.

Two cases involved disputes within the Soviet socialist regime,

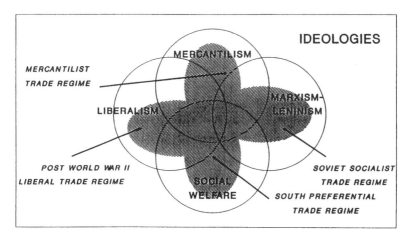

Figure 6-6. Multiple regime definition.

while several other cases involved Soviet socialist principles on one side and principles from another regime on the other side or sides. In six cases principles from all four regimes were articulated. One of these cases is isolated from the other five because sovereignty, rather than efficiency, was the post World War II principle at stake. Another interesting characteristic of this diagram is that all of the cases that escalated to become disputes fall below the indicated line, indicating that, even without specifically controlling for which problems cross the threshold of dispute initiation, disputes cluster together.

Patterns of norms. The similarity of trade problems based on their norms is shown in Figure 6-8. Here, the post World War II trade regime circumscribes almost all the cases. A few disputes are completely outside the post World War II trade regime; namely, two disputes that involve only the mercantilist norm of market regulation and the disputes that involve Soviet socialist, mercantilist, and South preferential norms.

Of particular interest here is the section on the right of the figure

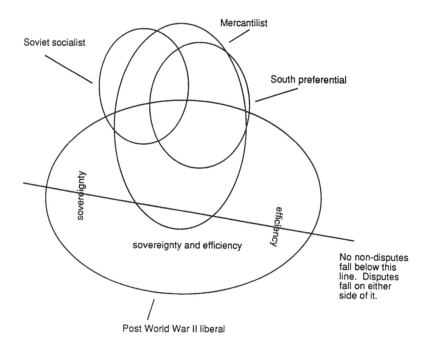

Figure 6-7. Similarities of cases based on principles.

where norms from the Soviet socialist, mercantilist, and South preferential trade regimes combine with norms from the post World War II liberal trade regime. Reciprocity, a post World War II norm seems to be often at odds with another post World War II norm, most favored nation status; with the Soviet socialist norm of state trading; with the South preferential norms of market regulation and redistribution of resources; and with the mercantilist norms of market regulation and protecting market shares. Reciprocity, therefore, emerges as a particularly contentious norm within the post World War II regime and across regimes.

In contrast, the post World War II norm of safeguards is a disputed issue primarily only within that regime, and even then it is not particularly contentious. Eleven of the seventeen cases that did not become disputes involve only the norm of safeguards. Whether or not safeguarding the domestic economy is legitimate is only problematic for the post World War II trade regime because in the other regimes the adherents assume that a primary goal of states is to safeguard their economies. In the post World War II trade regime, the right to safeguard a domestic economy is constrained. The limits of permissible safeguards, therefore, are contested within this regime.

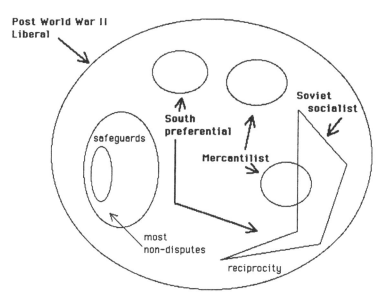

Figure 6-8. Similarities of cases based on norms.

Patterns of Rules. Figure 6-9 focuses on rules to show the similarities of cases of trade disputes and trade problems that did not escalate into disputes. Because I have coded 25 rules, the large number of combinations of rules makes this diagram more difficult to interpret. The areas shown identify disputes involving the more commonly referenced rules. Of these, three rules (the limitation on the use of technical standards, the limitation on the use of trade restrictions to rectify balance of trade problems, and reciprocity) are only contentious for trade problems within the post World War II liberal trade regime.

The remaining rules are shared by the post World War II trade regime and others. Special rights for developing countries is a rule included in the post World War II, Soviet socialist, and South preferential trade regimes. The rule allowing governments to protect certain vital sectors is shared by both the post World War II and mercantilist trade regimes. The rule prohibiting the use of subsidies is shared by the post World War II and Soviet socialist trade regimes.

Thirteen cases are represented by a small area on the right of the diagram. This is the most "dense" area of the map. It is also the area that shows the greatest penetration of different rules: the prohibition against subsidies, the legitimation of protection of certain vital sectors, and the requirement of reciprocity.

The cases that did not become disputes again tend to cluster together, though less prominently when the cases are mapped on the rules than on principles or norms. Of the thirteen cases in the most dense area, four are non-disputes. Of the five cases in the lower part of the area representing disputes over technical standards, four remained problems and did not become disputes. None of the seven problems found in the area representing disagreements involving, at least in part, balance of trade rules became disputes.

Discussion. Several main points emerge from looking at the similarities of principles, norms, and rules. First, the post World War II trade regime was the dominant trade regime between 1978 and 1983 (and is likely to continue to be so today). Second, some of its adherents disagree on the application and interpretation of its principles, norms, and rules. Third, the post World War II liberal trade regime is not the only regime. Fourth, since the adherents of different trade regimes interact with each other, trade disputes will often cross regime boundaries. When this happens, different beliefs about the principles, norms, and rules come to the fore.

These pictures show how the trade regimes intersect. Though they

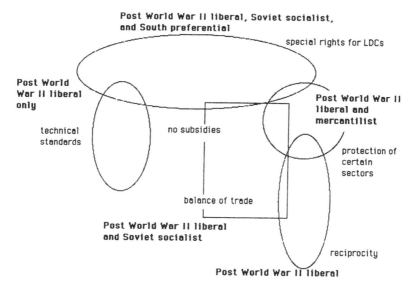

Figure 6-9. Similarities of cases based on rules.

are not as idealized as Figure 6-6, the pictures based on actual cases of trade problems support the hypotheses that regimes affect problem recognition and, more generally, that regimes account for both pattern and disorder in trade. The diagrams show intersecting regimes. The regimes do not stand alone. Moreover, principles, norms, and rules that, I have argued, are conceptually and ideologically distinct from the post World War II liberal trade regime do frame much of the debate about how agricultural trade should be conducted.

Appendix 3 contains the actual results from the MDS routines on each of these variables.

* * *

Identifying which regimes the participants in a trade dispute adhere to provides important keys to understanding why it is difficult to identify the boundaries of the trade disputes (or, more generally, trade problems). The way in which disputes are similar due to the participants, the issues, and the commodities or to the principles, norms, and rules reflects the way in which multiple contemporaneous regimes order trade. While the post World War II liberal trade regime is certainly dominant, it is not the sole system of principles, norms, rules, and decision-making procedures that is politically relevant. The mercantile and South preferential trade regime have also ordered some trade behavior, though advocates of the South preferential regime have been more successful at ordering political discourse about trade than at ordering trading *per se*. The Soviet socialist trade regime, as an important component of trade disputes between 1978 and 1983, is evident. This regime's precipitous decline raises interesting questions about which regimes will order trade in the immediate future.

NOTE

1. When I coded the information on the cases that are connected with each other for my data file, the limitations of the data processing required that I examine each case and list up to a fixed number of other cases that "overlapped" with it. I arbitrarily limited the number of "overlaps" to a maximum of five. If more than five cases seemed to be connected to the one I was coding, I recorded the five most closely connected. This operational definition is reflected in the Multi-Dimensional Scaling below. For this narrative, I have included all the cases that are connected to the sugar case.

Chapter 7

Conclusion

This book examined how regimes explain conflict as well as cooperation in agricultural trade. After identifying four trade regimes and where they come from, I explored their effects in food and feed trade disputes. Regimes matter, and differences between and within regimes help explain the intractability of agricultural trade disputes. The argument that multiple regimes explain cooperation *and* conflict pertains to other issues of international political economy as well. Understanding who is playing by which rules and where those rules come from—the foundational ideologies of the contemporary world —is essential for policy making in a turbulent, interdependent world. As a whole, the international trading system is characterized by orderly disorder. Order comes from the rules of the post World War II liberal, the mercantilist, and the South preferential trade regimes. Until recently, the Soviet socialist regime also ordered trade. Disorder comes from the interaction of actors adhering to different regimes and from the way these regimes overlap. Trade disputes and the public communication surrounding them are indicators of disorder.

Different sets of principles, norms, rules, and decision-making procedures offer alternative paradigms of proper trade behavior and even create the boundaries of trade as an issue area. Identifying whether a dispute involves the interpretation of an agreed rule or differing beliefs about what the rules should be allows us to explain dispute outcomes and processes. Moreover, analyzing how trade problems overlap with each other lets us look more critically at the expectations of the countries, producer groups, and firms. When the expectations of the participants differ, their negotiations are often unsuccessful, a relationship supported by this empirical investigation.

Power is certainly not absent from this equation. In past times when a single actor or small group of actors was able to maintain hegemonic control over the entire international trading system, the trade regime was imposed by the hegemon. Sixteenth to eighteenth century mercantilism is an example of such a period. Yet as the degree of hegemony enjoyed by the Western industrial powers (and particularly the US) is declining, and as alternate centers of political-economic strength are growing, smaller-scale regimes proliferate.

133

Policy makers may then choose their regimes according to their own boundedly rational decisions about the most advantageous set of trade rules for a given commodity. Still, the possible choices are limited by the ideologies and the histories that those ideologies have produced. Despite the revolutionary changes that have occurred in the former Soviet Union and its allies, conversion to capitalist organization of the domestic economy and post World War II liberal trade rules is a difficult and socially disruptive task. The reason is that it is hard to implement capitalism and liberal trade abruptly without having all the standard operating procedures that have developed over time in the West as capitalism and liberalism developed. Liberal procedures and institutions do not exist within the former Soviet Union because of its socialist history. Similarly, it would be almost inconceivable for the US suddenly to start adhering only to South preferental trade rules. Again the reason is that institutional habits are hard to break, even if the society reached a decision to change the ideology and attendant policies. Rules are sticky; they are hard to undo.

Multiple regimes for trade help explain the usually cooperative (if competitive) nature of trade, despite the diverse preferences of governments, firms, and other participants in the political arena of international commerce. Even in the area of agricultural trade, which has commonly been assumed to be unruled or at least less bound by the rules of the game than other kinds of trade, regimes can be seen to make a difference once distinct but contemporaneous sets of rules are identified. More importantly, multiple regimes help explain why simple trade problems become disputes, why differing definitions of the problem develop, and what happens in the conduct of a trade dispute. Taking this approach means that conflict in trade can be understood without postulating anarchy or regime decay. By providing a clearer understanding of the causes, consequences, and possible methods of resolving food and feed trade disputes in particular, this study has taken a small step toward removing the trade disputes that are one cause of food insecurity in the world.

EVALUATING THE MULTIPLE REGIME THEORY

In the first chapter, I used the theory of multiple, contemporaneous, and contending regimes to generate several hypotheses, which I then evaluated throughout the body of the book. The overarching proposition was: *Regimes interact with other political and economic factors to influence actors' perceptions, expectations, and behaviors in the recognition and conduct of trade disputes.* This proposition and the subsidiary hypotheses have been supported through an interpretation of the sugar trade dispute and through a combination of statistical hypothesis testing and interpretation using sixty-two cases of food and feed trade problems.

Of particular interest is the finding that the more a dispute is focused on regime questions (the pertinence of regimes to the dispute) the more hostile the dispute is likely to be. The expectations about behavior that regimes create also establish a standard for judging the violation of those expectations. This makes intuitive sense. If my neighbor has planted an apple tree near the line dividing his property from mine, in some jurisdictions I am entitled to the fruit that is growing on the branches that hang over my property. If I did not know that these apples were mine (after all, the tree *is* rooted on his land), I would not see anything amiss if my neighbor leaned over and picked the apples. But once I know that I have a right to those apples, a dispute could errupt if I found that the neighbor had harvested "my" fruit. Knowing the rules makes violations recognizable, and therefore the codification and institutionalization of regimes may increase conflict.

Overall, identifying the distinct trade regimes goes a long way toward explaining variation and similarity in the recognition and conduct of trade disputes. The theory links the ideological beliefs and preferences of policy makers with the broad patterns of what are primarily state-to-state negotiations. More importantly, this theory accounts for the behavior of policy makers as they speak and argue about trade—politick over trade—instead of relying on trade flows. The volume and direction of trade, though significant, tell more about the size and importance of the economies of Western industrial market economy countries than about why conflicts occur.

MULTIPLE REGIMES AND THE DECLINE OF SOVIET SOCIALISM

For a theoretical approach to trade conflict and cooperation to be truly robust, it must explain and predict even when apparently exogenous factors affect the complexity of international relations. Though revolutionary change within the Soviet bloc is exogenous to the model I have specified for explaining trade conflict and cooperation, the multiple regime theory lends itself to some very specific predictions about the likely tendency for trade within the now former Soviet bloc.

The organization of trade in these countries is rapidly changing, but the popular expectation that Eastern Europe has been converted to the free market is shortsighted. Prior to Gorbachev's reforms, the Soviet socialist trade regime provided a real, if mostly unnoticed, contemporary contrast to the dominant post World War II trade regime.

The legacy of the Soviet socialist trading system is a top-heavy, entrenched bureaucracy. Routinized procedures exist for centralized decision making, something inimical to post World War II liberal traders. When Soviet bloc countries traded, they employed long-term arrangements (LTAs). In the context of trade with non-CMEA countries, LTAs, agreements about how much will be supplied for how long, can be seen as a compromise between socialist and mercantilist rules. As such, they involved governments in the process of trade and limited fluctuations in the market. This procedure represents some commonality between the mercantilist and Soviet socialist regimes, despite the ideological divergence between them.

The recent rejection of Soviet socialist trade rules has presented an opportunity for questioning what ought to be the rules for trade and for the economic organization of the Eastern European countries. The result of rejecting the old rules without having a clear set of new ones leads to uncertainty. Political unrest is in part attributable to a lack of clear expectations about how the economies and trade of these countries will be ordered. Future political changes and the trade policies that result will have important effects on the organization of trade in the world.

The most likely outcome, given the structural complementarity between Soviet socialist and mercantilst economic organization, would be a transformation of these economies to a corporatist organization on the domestic side, coupled with mercantilist trade policy. This arrangement would put into place a system of prices to encourage more efficient production (something sorely needed in these countries) without having to eliminate the habit of significant government intervention into the economy. Quotas, voluntary export restraints, and similar agreements can be rationalized as necessary in order to get these economies on their feet. These will not, however, be short-term policies. The governments of Eastern Europe and the former Soviet Union do not share the tension inherent in Western embedded liberalism between the need to give up sovereign control over the economy in order to increase efficiency and the sovereign rights of states. In the former Soviet bloc, the state's role as organizer of the economy is deeply ingrained.

EXPECTATIONS ABOUT FUTURE INTERNATIONAL TRADE

The process of transforming the Soviet bloc into a mercantilist system is likely to be mirrored by a similar process in the industrialized North and the Newly Industrialized Countries. The reason for this expected trend lies in the relationship between power and the dominance of regimes. Historically, the dominant regime, the one that orders most of the trade, has been the one preferred by the most powerful state or group of states. As the power of the hegemon declines, policy makers from different countries will begin to assert claims based on other regimes more frequently.

Though some argue that the United States has not lost its hegemonic control over the international economy,[1] the United States no longer has the lead it once had over all other countries. It is the world's largest debtor, its productivity is not keeping pace with Japan and the European Community, and the poverty of its educational system bodes poorly for the future. We have entered the post-hegemonic age. But whether the loss of American hegemony is actual or only perceived by the majority of policy makers is unimportant. The perception of the loss of hegemony is sufficient to mark changes in the claims that are made about how trade should be conducted.

The post World War II liberal trade regime was so very successful for so very long because the United States, a hegemonic power, maintained it. As the strength of the United States relative to other countries decreases, there has been an increased urgency to the call for protectionism, voluntary export restraints, and negotiations over limiting access to the US market. A similar phenomenon seems to be happening in Europe as well.

The large European Community Market has been perceived as a major threat by US policy makers, who have countered with the US-Canada Free Trade Agreement and negotiations on a North American Free Trade Area. Ironically, the creation of free trade areas has a mercantile effect. Cutting the world up into large trading blocs has two major results. First, the poorest countries are extremely disadvantaged. Second, these blocs can argue with each other over the division of the inter-bloc market. The proliferation of bilateral agreements limiting access to markets and the whittling away of post World War II liberal principles by the creation of an essentially mercantilist Multi-Fiber Arrangement further points to this apparent trend toward a resurgence of mercantilism.

The potential dominance of the mercantile trade regime seems to be a reasonable expectation if we examine the domestic pressure for such a move and the mutual realization of policy makers in different countries that each much satisfy her or his domestic constituency. Mercantilist deal-cutting between policy makers seems a likely outcome. Such a procedure satisfies the demands of important interest groups in all the states concerned.

Finally, what will happen to the demands for a South preferential regime? The market regulation aspects of mercantile and South preferential trade are similar, even though their aims are different. I predict that the South will, of necessity, allow itself to be coopted into mercantile arrangements. Given a choice between entering negotiations and getting what little they can bargain for and boycotting negotiations and getting nothing, policy makers from developing countries will choose the former. Entering bargaining as a coalition will be the most effective tool these countries will have—the least bad, actually. This scenario has already been played out at the negotiations for the Multi-Fiber Arrangement. I predict there will be more of the same.

Individuals who advocate liberal, socialist, and South preferential trade regimes, along with the concommitant ideologies of liberalism, socialism, and social welfarism, will not disappear. People will continue to believe in and advocate the tenets of these ideologies. Some policy makers may continue to claim that trade should be conducted according to post World War II liberal, Soviet socialist, or South preferential rules. Multiple regimes will continue to exist, though the Soviet socialist trade regime is likely to peter out with the discrediting of the ideology of Soviet socialism.

New regimes, however, may emerge to challenge the entrenched regimes. It is possible to speculate that a regime based on the tenets of Islam may be advocated by policy makers of predominantly Moslem states, especially those in the Middle East. The economic power of oil-rich Arab countries is no longer under-estimated by the West, but Westerners continue to misunderstand the culture and ideology of Moslem society. One central principle that can be drawn from a cursory study of Islam is the primacy of the principle of caring for the community of Islam.

A cartel, an institution that would violate post World War II liberal requirements of efficiency through relatively free markets, is an extremely useful institution for securing the welfare of a pariticular community. In the case of the Arab oil producing countries, the obvious example is the Organization of Petroleum Exporting Countries, or more specifically, the Organization of Arab Petroleum Exporting Countries. The extremely hostile war between Iraq and Kuwait, though it was not caused soley by the dispute over oil export quotas, may represent some of the inherent conflict of regime creation. And, as the data in this study have suggested on a much smaller and less conflagratory scale, disputes over the content of regimes—which rules should there be, and when should a rule apply—can be quite hostile.

In the near term, however, I expect that mercantilism will replace liberalism as the dominant ideology generating the dominant trade regime. The new mercantilism differs from the old in some important ways. The old mercantilism came during the hegemony of Spain and later Britain. The new mercantilism is emerging during a period of declining hegemony. In the old Age of Mercantilism, Spain and Britain were able to impose trade rules. In the current era, coalitions of trading countries are forming to negotiate acceptable restrictions on trade and to divide market shares. Both periods share rules regarding the precedence given to the pursuit of national power and national wealth, the centralization of decisions about trade, and the inherent hierarchical organization of the international economic system.

A major assumption in all of this is the primacy of political expediency over liberal economic rationality or social welfare ideas of altruism. For this reason, I expect that a mercantilist trade regime will remain dominant until a new hegemon emerges, major political or economic upheavals undo the power of domestic interest groups, or—though this is rather utopian—governments come to accept an ethic of global responsibility and an ideology that embraces social welfare for all.

FOOD AND FEED TRADE IN A MERCANTILE WORLD

If the scenario I have outlined comes true, trade in food and feed may well become less overtly conflictual—but only because the limited power of the developing countries will not allow their policy makers to bring disputes to the international public agenda. When international agricultural trade is evaluated in terms of equity and market access, the developing countries that export agricultural commodities have the most to lose. The current Uruguay Round trade negotiations' stalemate centers, in large part, on the degree to which the United States and the European Community will continue to subsidize their agricultural sectors. Already, government support of farmers in the industrialized North has become an entitlement, one that protects farmers in the North, often at the expense of farmers in the South.

One effect of this mercantile trend is the exclusion of developing country producers from markets in the West. Another effect, especially for those Northern products that compete directly with products from the South (e.g., sugar), is continued oversupply and low prices in world markets. If commodity agreements in agriculture follow the example of the Multi-Fiber Arrangement, we can expect to see increasingly egregious discrimination against goods from the South. Agreements among more powerful countries to manage agricultural markets are likely to result in a diminished voice for developing countries in determining the conditions of those managed markets.

* * *

Regimes theory was developed when scholars set out to explain why, under realist assumptions of the world as a conflictual place, there was so much cooperation. These scholars found that regimes created the opportunity for rational inter-state cooperation. Agriculture, with the exception of specific commodity agreements, has usually been treated as unregulated by the GATT trade regime. My addition to this theory is that the explanatory power of regimes is even greater than has been assumed. In addition to explaining cooperation, regimes can explain conflict. But to understand how regimes are related to conflict and how food and feed trade is ordered by regimes, it is essential to recognize that regimes do not represent universally accepted definitions of an issue area nor universally accepted sets of principles, norms, rules and decision-making procedures. The important question is: Which participants in international affairs adhere to which regime grounded in which ideology? Careful attention to the politics of regimes can enrich our understanding of conflict and cooperation in a changing world.

NOTE

1. See, for example, Russett (1985) and Strange (1987).

Appendix 1

Compiling A Case Synopsis, Variable Operationalizations, and Coding

To further illustrate how I have constructed a case, I present here the text of a case synopsis. Since I use the sugar case in the main body of this book, I illustrate the process of compiling the synopsis with a different case, cocoa. The cocoa case is complex enough for most of the variables to be applicable. References to the problems of cocoa trade are arranged chronologically to create a case history. When a source is published only annually, I place references from the source at the end of the year it covers since these publications are actually put out after the year in the title. The citation at the end of the paragraph refers to the source in which I found the information. I use the section numbers when I explain the coding.

CASE SYNOPSIS

Cocoa, an important source of income for several developing countries such as the Ivory Coast, is subject to severe price fluctuations. Attempts have been made to control trade in cocoa through an international commodity agreement under the auspices of UNCTAD's Integrated Program for Commodities.

The First and Second International Cocoa Agreements contained two policy mechanisms for stabilizing prices within a predetermined band. The first method created export quotas to limit supply. Each country producing cocoa was allowed to export a set quantity of cocoa to the world market. The second method required the producing countries to hold and release buffer stocks as necessary to keep prices within the agreed upon range. When the price for cocoa went too low, the countries were required to purchase and store the cocoa to increase demand and raise prices. When the prices went too high, the countries were required to release their stocks to increase supply and lower prices.

Note that the export quota mechanism only controls supply, while

141

the buffer stock method intervenes in both supply and demand. Note too that export quotas, while limiting the amount of cocoa that a producer country can export, also give the country the *right* to export that amount. The buffer stock mechanism is a more market oriented instrument because it does not set limits on a country's exports.

In 1978, the Second International Cocoa Agreement, enacted in 1975, was due to expire. The cocoa dispute, like the sugar dispute, revolves around what shape a new Agreement should take.

§1 In March 1978, the Executive Council of the International Cocoa Council met and was unable to reach an agreement over whether the Cocoa Agreement should be renegotiated. The Council authorized an *ad hoc* committee to examine the matter further. From 12 to 16 June 1978, the Cocoa Council meeting was convened, and it was announced that the *ad hoc* committee would report to the Council on 24-28 July. The current agreement was to expire on 30 September 1979 unless it was extended.

The US did not join the 1975 Agreement because it thought the plan too rigid. The 1975 Agreement was using export quotas and buffer stocks to keep prices in line, but there had not yet been a test of the system's effectiveness. As an example, in the summer of 1978 the price of cocoa remained high despite the absence of buffer stocks. At the Council's request, the US participated in the negotiations as an observer and would submit a position paper. The US plan for a new agreement would replace the current export quota/buffer stock system with a more flexible one relying solely on buffer stocks. In the US plan, prices would be stabilized within a band, the size of buffer stocks would be limited, and the accumulation or disposal of buffer stocks would be constrained.

The countries that produce cocoa, in contrast, believed that cocoa prices in the 1975 Agreement were too low and needed rapid adjustment. All sides, however, saw the need for a simple, flexible mechanism for intervention. The decision on whether to renegotiate would come in July **(*Foreign Agriculture*, 3 July 1978)**.

§2 A European Community document reports that the preparatory meeting for the Third International Cocoa Agreement examined proposals for a simpler, less rigid Agreement, which, in contrast to the First and Second Agreements, would not be based on export quotas and the operation of international buffer stocks related to different price levels. The Preparatory Committee focused on the use of buffer stocks as the main instrument for market stabilization, though there are varying opinions from the exporting and importing countries about intervention, the nature of buffer stocks, and the price review arrangements. According to this source, "the question of the size and financing of the stock is not giving rise to any serious difficulties" (*Bulletin of the European Communities*, **10-1978**).

§3 The FAO's *State of Food and Agriculture, 1978* examines the situation of international markets for agricultural goods. The report singles out the problem of unstable prices, including those of cocoa; and problems of access to markets for cocoa producers. Progress, the report states, was slow on the implementation of the Integrated Program for Commodities, of which the International Cocoa Agreement is part (**FAO, 1978**).

§4 On 18 January 1979, the European Community transmitted to the EC Council its recommendation for a decision on the scheduled negotiation (29 January to 23 February) of the Third International Cocoa Agreement. The report, which does not discuss the details of the recommendation, notes that the Draft Agreement differs radically from the First and Second Agreements in that the proposed Third Agreement is to be simpler and based essentially on an international buffer stock. The report notes that the EC is the world's largest importer of cocoa, and cocoa is a major agricultural commodity for the developing countries (*Bulletin of the European Communities*, **1-1979**).

§5 An EC document notes the failure of the 29 January to 23 February negotiations to reach a satisfactory conclusion because of differences regarding the prices determining buffer stock operations. Progress was made on many economic and administrative provisions of the draft Agreement. The producer countries want to set minimum prices at US $1.86 per pound, a figure based on the production costs of the Ivory Coast. The consumer countries want to start with the foreseeable price levels for 1980-81, estimated at an average of $0.90 to $0.95 per pound. Higher prices, the consumer countries suggest, have led to the use of cocoa substitute. A date for resumption of the talks would be set (*Bulletin of the European Communities*, **2-1979**).

§6 Another negotiating meeting was held from 16 July to 2 August 1979, and although there were not concrete results, some progress had been made. There was "considerable narrowing of the wide differences of opinion" dividing the importers and the exporters, according to an EC publication. The EC, the report states, was taking "an active and influential part in these negotiations." The report concludes that more progress still needs to be made (*Bulletin of the European Communities, 7/8-1979*).

§7 According to the Soviet publication, *Foreign Trade*, the failure of the Commodity Programs was a result of

(1) the imperialist powers' competition becoming "more sophisticated and camouflaged;"

(2) capitalist trade leading to "unequal economic relations, a policy of coercion and uncontrolled exploitation of developing countries . . . and vast speculation which profits . . . the multinational corporations that control quite a large chunk of the developing countries' trade in primary materials;"

(3) the monopolies' plunder of the developing countries;

(4) the US's real goal of ensuring "unobstructed operations" of the monopolies;

(5) the EC's expansionist and protectionist policies;

(6) the insistence of the West that there be independent standing research groups; and

(7) a lack of consensus among the developing countries.

The US, according to the publication, "is not averse to international agreements where there is a certain degree of (US) governmental control, but is opposed to any agreement where this is absent." Divisions among developing countries, both producers and exporters, contributed to the problem, according to *Foreign Trade* (*Foreign Trade*, 5-1979).

§8 *Foreign Trade* includes an article on "Specific Features of the Cocoa Market Today" in February 1982. The article notes that the Soviet Union was a major cocoa importer, as were the US, the Federal Republic of Germany, the UK, and France. This article stresses the role of monopolies in controlling cocoa trade. "Practically all cocoa used in making confectionery in the capitalist world is, in the final count, purchased and processed by several international monopolies, the leading ones being General Foods, Hershey Foods, Nestle SA, Rowintree Mackintosh, Mars, Cadbury, Schweppes, TriumfSchokoladefabrik GmbHy and Interfood SA. These monopolies in some measure control cocoa-bean processing in the producing countries as well."

The article predicts that if the supply of cocoa continued low and the prices remained high, the trend for substituting non-cocoa products for cocoa would increase. In the 1970s, there had been an increase in the export market share for cocoa of West European non-producing countries, especially the Netherlands and West Germany. According to the Soviet source, "monopolies' inter-subsidiary shipments account for a considerable portion of these exports from industrial capitalist countries."

The article continues to state that industrialized capitalist countries were the main cocoa importers. Their share had declined from 82.2% in 1970 to 80.2% in 1977 because of market saturation, low population growth, the use of fillers and substitutes, prohibitive tariffs, and non-tariff barriers, especially in the EC. Cocoa bean prices would always be inherently unstable because of weather, speculation, social, political, military, and other chance and temporary factors. While hedging could give some stability to the market, in the long run "it would be in the interests of both consumers and producers to have a new effective International Cocoa Agreement."

Although the 29 January to 23 February Working Meeting on Cocoa failed to come to some agreement, in June 1979 the participants agreed on $1.20 per pound price minimum. In the February meeting, the exporting countries wanted a much higher minimum price and a much smaller difference between the maximum and minimum price than that which the importers wanted. According to the Soviet source, the narrow band would hamper operations of the stabilizing stock because of highly volatile prices (*Foreign Trade*, **2-1980**).

§9 The FAO's *State of Food and Agriculture 1979* notes that the International Cocoa Agreement was extended to March 1980, but has since (by the 1980 publication date of this source) lapsed due to failure to agree on price levels (**FAO, 1979**).

§10 According to *Foreign Agriculture*, the International Cocoa Agreement collapsed on 31 March 1980. The Ivory Coast and Brazil, two producing countries, subsequently tried to spearhead the drive for a producer cartel. This effort was not likely to succeed because of lower demand and greater supplies of cocoa. The Agreement collapsed because participants could not agree upon the new price range target that reflected market prices.

The Ivory Coast and Brazil held out for maintaining prices in a range from $1.20 to $1.66 per pound. Most consumer countries favored a range of $1.00 to $1.46 per pound. During the past several years, the cocoa prices under the International Cocoa Agreement had been maintained in a range from $0.65 to $0.81 per pound. The US, which was not a signatory to the International Cocoa Agreement but which is the largest single country consumer, did participate in the negotiations (*Foreign Agriculture*, **June 1980**).

§11 In the Report of the Committee on Commodities to the ninth session of the UNCTAD Trade and Development Board, 29 September to 7 October 1980, the representative of the Committee noted that the unsuccessful renegotiation of the Agreement was due to a lack of agreement on prices. He urged governments to take action since prices had since fallen to their lowest level since 1976. The representative of the EC, to correct statements about its import policy, noted that cocoa, as well as other commodities, were not subject to import levies. Only customs duties were imposed **(UNCTAD/Trade and Development Board, 29 September to 7 October 1980; TD/B/834; TD/B/C.1/218).**

§12 The report of the Ad Hoc Intergovernmental Committee for the Integrated Program for Commodities on its tenth session, 27 October 1980, records the comments of the meeting's participants. The chairman of the Committee noted that if the pending renegotiation of the International Cocoa Agreement failed to lead to a renewal, it would be a serious setback for the entire Integrated Program. The spokesman for the Group of 77 stated that it has not been possible to agree on a remunerative and equitable minimum price for cocoa. The representative of China maintained that the major obstacle to the implementation of the IPC was the activities of international monopolistic capitalists who, proceeding from an attitude of maintaining the old international economic order, lack the will to implement the Program.

The spokesman for Group B (the industrialized market economy countries), disagreed; progress toward implementation of the IPC had undoubtedly been made. Japan's representative agreed. Contrary to the report made by the UNCTAD secretariat, considerable progress had been made on the IPC. He did not share the view that efforts toward the conclusion of commodity agreements had not yielded satisfactory results. However, except for cocoa, coffee, sugar, tin, and natural rubber, there had been no agreement about whether pricing measures, including stocking, would be suitable.

Although the Ad Hoc Committee's work had come to an end, remarked the chairman, their task had not been completed. The progress which had been made was inadequate, but was also considerable toward advancing the objectives of the IPC **(UNCTAD/Trade and Development Board, 27 October 1980; TD/B/IPC/AC/35).**

§13 In January 1981, an article in *Foreign Agriculture* suggests that world cocoa bean output is likely to continue to increase during the decade. The Ivory Coast is the world's top producer. Production has increased, but consumption has decreased. The New International Cocoa Agreement was approved recently in Geneva, but the Ivory Cost and the US elected not to join. The Agreement's objective is to stabilize cocoa bean prices between $1.10 and $1.50 per pound through the use of buffer stocks (*Foreign Agriculture*, **January 1981**).

§14 Because the International Cocoa Organization failed to reach the required membership quotas for operation (80% for exporters and 70% for importers), the organization extended the 31 May deadline for joining to 30 September 1981. By 31 May, 72% of exporting countries and 45% of importing countries had made provisional membership applications. The Ivory Coast and the US still had not joined (*Foreign Agriculture*, **July 1981**).

§15 The Soviet Union's *Foreign Trade* notes that the Third International Cocoa Agreement of November 1980 reflected the capitalists' interests with respect to the price mechanism. Export quotas were abandoned in favor of complete reliance on buffer stocks (*Foreign Trade 8-1981*).

§16 The 1981 *State of Food and Agriculture* reports the slow progress in setting up institutions for expanding and stabilizing trade in agricultural commodities. This was a cause for concern. The commodity negotiations being conducted under the Integrated Program for Commodities were disappointing (**FAO, 1981**).

§17 The report of the UNCTAD Committee on Commodities on its first special session, 8 to 12 February 1982, includes statements dealing with the International Cocoa Agreement. In the view of industrialized market economy countries, the Agreement of 1980 had come into effect and was beginning to set up the buffer stock. Financing for the buffer stock was being worked out. Switzerland's representative noted his country's support for the Agreement and hoped that it would stabilize prices and thereby increase the prosperity of the world cocoa economy, particularly of the producing countries that depend so heavily on cocoa. Unfortunately, the industrialized market economy countries' report continued, the weak participation in the agreement had led to disappointing results in the market. This was especially due to the failure of the largest producers and consumers to join.

Ecuador's representative noted that it was important that the country which was a main producer of cocoa and the country that was a main consumer should accede to the Agreement. Egypt's representative noted that the cocoa market was characterized by oligopolistic buyers **(UNCTAD/Trade and Development Board; 8-12 February 1982; TD/B/894)**.

§18 A report by the UNCTAD secretariat notes that the Tokyo Round of the Multilateral Trade Negotiations of the GATT resulted in a reduced tariff on Japanese imports of cocoa, which indicates reduced effective protection for the processed product **(UNCTAD/ Trade and Development Board, 18 February 1982; TD/B/885)**.

§19 In a document prepared by the UNCTAD secretariat and presented to the Trade and Development Board of UNCTAD, tenth session, 26 January to 8 February 1983, it is noted that cocoa prices had declined since 1980 and that the International Cocoa Agreement had activated its economic provisions. The Agreement could not stop all the downward price moves, but it had been able to give some relief to the exporting countries in a time of recession. Cocoa prices went down because of oversupply. High interest rates, which raised the costs of stockholding, also pushed prices down. The Cocoa Agreement had been less successful at controlling prices than the Coffee Agreement. The Coffee Agreement was based on export quotas, though the burden of stock holding fell on the exporting countries **(UNCTAD/Trade and Development Board, 26 January-8 February 1983; TD/B/944; TD/B/C.1/247)**.

OPERATIONALIZATION OF THE VARIABLES AND CODING

One way to look for the trade dispute patterns that a multiple regime theory would predict is to examine several trade disputes. Since I am looking at 62 cases, too many to compare discursively, coding the salient variables allows me both to keep track of those I will discuss descriptively and to use quantitative methods for description and hypothesis testing as appropriate.

Coding the kind of information contained in my case synopses can be a particularly opaque way to analyze data. In this section, I reprint my coding questions for variables I use in the analysis and describe the coding process, using the cocoa case as an example. The section numbers refer to the sections in the case synopsis that I used when making a coding decision.

Dependent Variables

Was a dispute initiated?

A problem (i.e., the recognition in a public source that there is an issue to be talked or written about) becomes initiated as a dispute when one or more international actors *disagrees*, in a public arena through official statement or action, with a specific trade policy of one or more other actors.

A dispute is initiated by an event. An event occurs when one actor does something to one or more other actors.

The cocoa case was initiated as a dispute (evidence: §1, §3, §7, §8, et al.). In this case, the complaints highlight the way in which cocoa is traded and how that trade is managed.

Level of hostility and cooperation

Looking at the most conflictual action, what was the intensity level of this action?

I omitted this variable for cases that were not initiated as disputes. The intensity scale is a measure of how conflictive or cooperative the interaction among the sides to the dispute is. (Compare Azar, 1980.) The maximum and minimum intensity level describe the conflictual range of the dispute. Below is a description of each of the intensity scale values.

(1) Most cooperative. Action expresses extreme good will and excellent relations between the parties.

(2) Action represents a somewhat more cooperative position held by at least one side.

(3) Action shows a small lessening of tension or propensity to be cooperative by at least one side.

(4) Neutral.

(5) Action reflects tension between the sides or propensity to be conflictive by at least one side.

(6) Action reflects strong disagreement between the sides. Retaliation is likely to seem imminent.

(7) Most conflictive. Action reflects as high a degree of hostility as possible within the context of a trade dispute. Retaliatory actions fall into this category.

The intensity of the most hostile action in the cocoa case was the most conflictive level: 7. (Evidence: Attempting to form a cartel falls into the most conflictive category because it negates the multilateral approach of the Integrated Program for Commodities. Threatening to form a cartel would have rated a 6.)

Looking at the most cooperative action, what was the intensity level of this action?

I omitted this variable for cases that were not initiated as disputes. The intensity of this action was a show of increased willingness to cooperate by at least one of the participants, scored as intensity level 2 (evidence: the Third International Cocoa Agreement of November 1980).

Success of negotiation and mediation

How successful were the multilateral negotiations?

I omitted this variable for cases that were not initiated as disputes. If the negotiations led to a resolution of the dispute, then I coded this variable as very successful. If the negotiations led to some progress toward resolution (the intensity level of the actions taken by the participants declined), but did not result in resolution of the actors' differences, I coded the success as moderate. If no progress was made, then I coded the negotiations as not successful.

The multilateral negotiations over cocoa trade were moderately successful (evidence: §17).

There was no mediator in the cocoa case. Had their been one or more (the structure of the data file allows me to collect data for up to four mediators), I would have judged how successful the mediators were.

Dispute Outcome

What was the outcome of the dispute?

I omitted this variable for cases that were not initiated as disputes. I declared a particular side the winner if its claims were accepted, on the whole, as correct and if its demands were, for the most part, met. "No side lost" means that all (or both) sides won some concessions and made some concessions.

In the cocoa case, my judgement was that Side 1 won the dispute (evidence: §19). I made this determination because the new Agreement was unable to keep prices from falling. Side 1 is composed of consumer countries that benefit from lower prices.

At the end of the dispute, or at the end of 1983 if the dispute continued past 1983, was Side 1 satisfied with the outcome?

I omitted this variable for cases that were not initiated as disputes. I answered this question by interpreting the extent to which the side's goals, as articulated or inferred, were achieved in the outcome of the dispute.

I judged that Side 1 was moderately satisfied with the outcome because it achieved some of its goals. (Evidence: I inferred that the consumer countries, which adhere to the post World War II liberal trade regime, would have preferred that there be no Agreement, but at least the new Agreement relied solely on buffer stocks and did not require export quotas.)

I asked the same question for the other sides.

I judged Side 2 to be moderately satisfied with the result of the case as well. (Evidence: The producing countries that wanted a new Agreement got one, but they didn't get everything they wanted. This is especially the case since the US and the Ivory Coast, the largest consumer and producer countries, respectively, were able to prevent the effective implementation of the agreement.) I judged Side 3 to be dissatisfied with the result, based on interpretations of Soviet rhetoric (evidence: §15).

To what degree were all sides satisfied by the outcome of the dispute or by the end of 1983 if the dispute continued past 1983?

I omitted this variable for cases that were not initiated as disputes.

I judged the overall satisfaction to be mixed (evidence: level of satisfaction coded for each side).

Main Independent Variables

Regime Adherence; Principles, Norms, and Rules; and Regime Pertinence

What is the dominant regime on Side 1?

I coded the regime which I thought best described the actors' rhetoric on trade, unless there was evidence that the actors' deeds did not coincide with their words. I evaluated how closely the actors adhered to that regime as well.

In the cocoa case, Side 1 represents statements primarily consistent with the post World War II liberal trade regime. Adherence is strong.

What is the central principle at issue in this dispute, according to Side 1?

I attempt to determine the most important principle, based (if there is disagreement) on the position of the primary actor on the side. The principle must be consistent with the principles of the side's regime. (I followed the same procedure to determine norm and rule.)

The principle invoked by Side 1 is efficiency (evidence: §2, §13).

What is the central norm at issue in this dispute, according to Side 1?

The norm invoked by Side 1 is the Generalized System of Preferences (evidence: willingness to negotiate an agreement preferentially beneficial to developing countries).

What is the central rule at issue in this dispute, according to Side 1?

The rule invoked by Side 1 is the provision granting special rights to developing countries (evidence: willingness to negotiate an agreement preferentially beneficial to developing countries).

I ask the same questions about regimes for Sides 2 and 3.

Side 2 adheres very strongly to the South preferential regime (evidence: attempt to regulate trade through an international institution). The principle invoked by Side 2 is stability of prices (evidence: §19) and the norm is market regulation (evidence: the structure of the agreement). The rule invoked by Side 2, like that of

Side 1, is the granting of special rights to developing countries. It makes sense for the two sides, adhering to different regimes, to invoke the same rule because the rules of different regimes overlap.

Side 3 adheres very strongly to the Soviet socialist regime (evidence: rhetoric regarding commodity markets and imperialism was consistent for all commodities I examined). The norm invoked by Side 3 is state trading (evidence: §8). The principle invoked is anti-imperialism (evidence: §7, §8). The rule invoked is the need to impose controls on the operations of monopolies (evidence: §8).

How pertinent are regime-oriented themes to the case?

When coding this variable, I considered explicit references to regime principles, norms, rules, or procedures. I also looked for practices that implied unstated assumptions about proper trade behavior. For example, a case involving the simple mention of a change in tariff laws without comment on whether those changes are justified or proper would not pertain much to regime-oriented themes. On the other extreme, a case involving discussions about when governments should intervene in markets strongly pertains to regime issues.

In the case of cocoa trade, the pertinence of regime issues to the content of the case is very high because the case centers around whether to create and, if so, how to structure a South preferential commodity agreement.

How many regimes were represented among the sides?

Three regimes were represented in this case.

Other Independent Variables

Relative Economic and Political Power

Which side is the strongest economically?

I omitted this variable if no single side was appreciably stronger than the other. The differences in economic strength had to be obvious. When I was uncertain, I looked at the GNP per capita for the measure of economic strength. The differences, to be coded, had to be "order of magnitude" differences. For example, I coded the US, the EC, and Japan as equally strong on the economic scale.

Side 1 (the US plus the EC plus Switzerland) was the side which was strongest economically (evidence: *UN Statistical Yearbook*).

Which side is strongest in terms of political/military power?

This variable is analogous to the one measuring differences in economic strength. Again, I code only large differences in power. I would, for example, consider the US and the Soviet Union as being of equal power.

In this case, Side 1 and Side 3 were equally strong in political/military terms. (Evidence: US and the Soviet Union, the primary actors on Sides 1 and 3, are of roughly equal political/military strength.)

Overall Level of Friendliness

Aside from tensions caused by this problem, how can the relations between the sides be characterized?

I coded this variable in broad terms, using general knowledge of the relations among states between 1978 and 1983.

Relations between the sides were a combination of neutral, friendly, and unfriendly. (Evidence: Relations between Side 1— the US, the EC, and Switzerland—and Side 2—Ivory Coast, Brazil, and Ecuador—are neutral or friendly; relations between Side 1 and Side 3—the Soviet Union—are neutral or unfriendly; relations between Side 2 and Side 3 are neutral or friendly.)

Importance of agriculture

What percent of GDP does agriculture represent for the primary actor on Side 1?

Originally, I planned to include a variable representing the percentage of total imports (or exports) which the commodity at issue accounted for in the trade of the primary actor on Side 1. These data were not consistently available from standard UN or FAO sources, however. Instead, I measured the dependence of the actor on agriculture. I used data from the *UN Statistical Yearbook*. I looked for the information for the year prior to the beginning of the case. If this information was not available, I used the closest date possible. I did not code this variable if the primarily actor on the side was not a nation-state.

The proportion of the US GDP attributed to agriculture was 3 percent (evidence: *UN Statistical Yearbook*).

These questions were also asked for each of the other sides.

Side 2 was primarily an exporter of cocoa, and the proportion of the Ivory Coast's GDP attributed to agriculture was 26 percent. The Soviet Union was primarily an importer, and its share of GDP attributed to agriculture was 17 percent (evidence: *UN Statistical Yearbook*).

Number of participants

How many actors are there in total?

The total number of actors was seven.

The seven actors were aligned on three sides. A side consists of at least one actor with a unique policy position on the dispute. It is possible for different actors from one nation (e.g., the government and a group of producers) to be on different sides. To the extent that I can determine which side is complaining and which side's policies sparked the complaint, I label the side of the primary defendant *Side 1*. That is, when the problem is articulated, the actors on Side 1 will be the ones charged with violating international rules of the game. *Side 2* will be the side raising the issue. *Sides 3 and 4* will represent other defendant and/or plaintiff points of view. There must be at least two sides to the dispute. Most studies of conflict assume that a dispute has only two sides, but not all conflicts can be neatly divided into Us versus Them. Theoretically, there may be as many sides as there are variations on positions of the participants. Practical concerns about the data file lead me to limit the number of sides to four. In compiling the case synopses I did not see any cases that clearly had a fifth side.

How many actors are there on Side 1?

There are three actors on Side 1: the US, the EC, and Switzerland (evidence: §8, §17).

These questions are then repeated for Sides 2 and 3.

Side 2 includes the Ivory Coast (primary actor), Brazil, and Ecuador (evidence: §10, §17). The Soviet Union was Side 3 (evidence: §7). A single actor composed Side 3.

Institutions

Did all the participants in the dispute belong to a formal organization which had procedures for trade dispute conciliation?

Such an organization did exist (evidence: UNCTAD).

Overlap variables

Overlaps

How many cases overlapped with this case?

I coded a maximum of five overlapping cases. An overlapping case is one which is related to this case because of the actors, the commodity, or the general issue area involved. When I identified a case as overlapping the case I was coding, I had a subjective sense that the overlapping cases are related by commodity, issue, or actors and that the outcome of the one case would affect the outcome of the other.

The cocoa case overlaps with the following cases:

(1) Soviet complaints about the international trading system;

(2) the dispute over international coffee trade;

(3) the dispute over the International Wheat and Grain Agreement;

(4) the dispute over trade in oils, oilseeds, and fats; and

(5) the dispute over international sugar trade.

(Evidence: Cocoa is one commodity referred to in the case concerning Soviet complaints about the international trading system. Also, the latter four cases are all issues being negotiated under the Integrated Program for Commodities.)

Appendix 2

Description of the Data

This appendix describes the distributions of the variables that provide general information about the data and of the variables used in the data analysis.

Table A2-1. Cases

AUSTRALIAN BARRIERS TO IMPORTS: US and EC complaints about Australia's barriers to imports of several products.

AUSTRALIAN EXPORT POLICIES: US concerns over Australian exports of several commodities.

AUSTRIA: US concern over Austria's proposed protection of wheat and coarse grain producers by taxing oilseed products.

BENELUX: US complaints about these countries' requirements that meat imports must weigh at least 3 kg.

BRAZIL: US concerns over Brazil's restrictions on imports (especially apples and pears) due to balance of payments problems.

EC-CANADIAN TRADE RELATIONS: Disagreements between the EC and Canada over the countervailing tariffs imposed by Canada following reclassification by the EC of tariffs on unwrought lead and zinc.

CANADIAN-US TRADE ISSUES: Disagreements between the US and Canada over trade in several products, including poultry, eggs, and cheese.

COLOMBIA: US complaints over Columbia's import licensing requirements.

EC BARRIERS TO TRADE: Complaints about EC barriers to trade, including tariffs, quotas, variable levies, taxes, licensing arrangements, and technical requirements.

EC DISCRIMINATION—US CITRUS: US complaints over EC preferential imports of citrus products from the Mediterranean Associates.

EC DISCRIMINATION—CANADIAN BEEF: Canadian complaints over EC refusal to recognize Canadian beef ratings while the EC accepts USDA ratings.

157

EC EXPANSION: US and other countries' complaints stemming from proposed and actual rule changes designed to ease the accession of new members to the EC.

EC SUBSIDIES: Complaints over the EC's export and producer subsidies.

ECUADOR'S BARRIERS TO IMPORTS: US concerns over import limitations imposed because of Ecuador's balance of payments problems.

EGYPTIAN BARRIERS TO IMPORTS: US concerns over Egyptian barriers to imports, particularly of poultry and poultry products. Egypt's policy is geared toward making the country more self-reliant.

FINLAND'S, CANADA'S, AND SWEDEN'S PESTICIDE REGULATIONS: US complaints about low allowable levels of pesticide residues in horticultural exports to these countries.

HONG KONG-FRENCH TRADE RELATIONS: Hong Kong's retaliation against quotas imposed by France on imports of Hong Kong quartz watches.

INDONESIAN BARRIERS TO IMPORTS: US concerns over Indonesian barriers to imports for several food products.

JAPAN'S RESTRICTIONS ON IMPORTS: Complaints against Japan's import quotas and other restrictions on imports.

JAPANESE SUBSIDIZED EXPORTS: Complaints against Japan's subsidization of rice exports.

MALAYSIAN BARRIERS TO IMPORTS: US concerns over technical barriers to trade and barriers to trade designed to protect domestic industry.

MEXICO AND US FARMERS: US farmers' complaints over imports of Mexican produce.

MOROCCO: US concerns over Morocco's limits on imports as a result of balance of payment problems.

NIGERIA: US concerns over Nigeria's restrictions on imports due to balance of payments problems.

PERUVIAN TRADE POLICIES: US concerns about Peru's limitations on poultry and wheat imports.

PRC-US AGRICULTURAL TRADE: Efforts to expand Chinese-American agricultural trade and attempts to resolve problems which arise.

SINGAPORE'S NON-TARIFF BARRIERS: US concerns over technical restrictions which limit imports of processed food.

SOUTH KOREA: US concerns over South Korea's restrictions on agricultural imports.

SPANISH EXPORT SUBSIDIES: US concerns about Spanish export subsidies on several goods.

SWISS IMPORT POLICY: Concerns about Swiss protection of domestic producers and attempts to improve its level of self-sufficiency.

SYRIAN IMPORT POLICY: US concerns about regulatory requirements for exports to Syria.

THAI IMPORT CONTROLS: US concerns about Thailand's restrictions on imports of feed ingredients and duties on other agricultural products.

US EXPORT POLICIES: EC concerns over US exports of dairy, wheat, flour, and feed ingredients.

US IMPORT POLICY: Complaints by the EC, the Soviet Union, and other countries about US import policy for several products.

US-LATIN AMERICAN TRADE RELATIONS: US concerns about import restrictions imposed by Latin American countries and the workings of the Andean Pact.

US RESTRICTIONS ON IMPORTS OF SUGAR FROM NICARAGUA: Nicaragua's charge that trade embargo for political purposes is not legitimate.

VENEZUELAN IMPORT POLICIES: US concerns about Venezuela's import restraints imposed because of balance of payments and economic safeguards problems.

ALMONDS: US almond growers complaints about India's licensing procedures for importing almonds.

APPLES 1: Disagreement between Chile and the EC over the EC's imposition of a quota on imports of Chilean apples.

APPLES 2: Disagreement between Taiwan and the US over Taiwan's restrictions on apple imports.

APPLES 3: Norwegian restrictions on apple imports.

BANANAS: Multilateral disagreement over banana trade.

COCOA: Multilateral attempts to renegotiate the International Cocoa Agreement.

COFFEE1: Multilateral disagreement over coffee trade.

COFFEE2: Disagreement between Spain and Brazil over Spain's tariff classification of coffee imports.

DAIRY: Multilateral disagreement over dairy trade.

EC POLICY ON IMPORTS OF FEED GRAINS AND NON-GRAIN FEED SUBSTITUTES: Multilateral disagreement over EC restrictions on imports of feed ingredients.

FLOUR: Multilateral disagreement on flour trade.

FRUIT AND VEGETABLES: Multilateral disagreement on fruit trade.

INTERNATIONAL DISPUTE OVER THE INTERNATIONAL WHEAT/ GRAIN AGREEMENT: Multilateral disagreement over the renegotiation of the International Wheat Agreement.

NEGOTIATIONS ON AN INTERNATIONAL MEAT AGREEMENT: Multilateral disagreement over the formulation of an international meat agreement.

OILSEEDS, OILS, AND FATS: Multilateral disagreement over trade in oilseeds, oils, and fats.

POULTRY AND EGGS: Multilateral disagreement over trade in poultry products, particularly concerning subsidized exports of chicken.

RICE: Multilateral disagreement over rice trade.

SHEEPMEAT: New Zealand's and other exporting countries' concerns over EC restrictions on sheepmeat imports.

SUGAR: Multilateral disagreement over the renegotiation of the International Sugar Agreement.

TEA: Multilateral disagreement over the formulation of an International Tea Agreement.

US MEAT IMPORT AGREEMENTS: Concerns over US meat import arrangements.

WINES AND SPIRITS: Multilateral disagreement over trade in wines and spirits.

SOVIET BLOC/NON-SOVIET BLOC TRADE: Concerns over trade between CMEA members and non-CMEA members.

INTRA-CMEA DISPUTES: Concerns among the CMEA members over trade within the bloc.

PRC-CMEA TRADE: Concerns over expansion of trade between the PRC and the Soviet bloc.

ACTORS

Table A2-2. States

Anti-Export Quota Banana Exporting Countries	Argentina	Australia	Austria
Belgium	Brazil	Bulgaria	Chile
Colombia	Ecuador	Egypt	Finland
France	Group of 77 Developing Countries	Hungary	India
Indonesia	Ivory Coast	Japan	LAFTA Andean Pact Countries
Luxembourg	Malaysia	Mediterranean Associates of the EC	Mexico
Morocco	The Netherlands	New Zealand	Nicaragua
Nigeria	Non-EC Industrialized Market Economy Countries	Norway	"Other" Coffee Consuming Countries
"Other" Coffee Exporting Countries	"Other" GATT Members	"Other" Soviet Bloc Countries	People's Republic of China
Peru	Philippines	Pro-Export Quota Banana Exporting Countries	Republic of China (Taiwan)
Rumania	Singapore	South Africa	South Korea
Countries of the Southern Hemisphere	Spain	Sweden	Switzerland
Syria	Tea Exporting Countries	Thailand	Union of Soviet Socialist Republics
United States of America	Uruguay	Venezuela	Yugoslavia

Table A2-3. Non-State Actors

Common Market European Community	Subnational Producer Groups **Australia:**	Subnational Producer Groups (continued)	Transnational Producer Groups **EC:**
	Fruit Canning Industry	**United States:** California Almond Growers	Apple Growers Farmers
International Organizations Food and Agriculture Organization	**Federal Republic of Germany:** Farmers	Citrus Growers	Feed Firms *Multinational Corporations*
Latin American Free Trade Association	Feed Firms **France:**	Florida Growers Grape Growers	Fruit Marketing, US-based Multinational Corporations
UN Commission on Trade and Development	Growers **Hong Kong:** Watch Manufacturers	Great Western Sugar Meat Industry	
	Mexico: Cattle Farmers	Pacific Northwest Apple Industry	
		Peach Growers	
		Soy Growers	

Table A2-4. Number of Actors on Each Side

	FREQUENCIES			
Number of Actors	Main Plaintiffs Side 1	Main Defendants Side 2	Other Participants Side 3	Other Participants Side 4
1	44	34	9	6
2	7	11	5	2
3	6	5	0	1
More than 3	5	12	9	1

ACTIONS

Table A2-5. Types of Most Cooperative and Hostile
Actions

Action	Frequency
HOSTILE ACTIONS	
Complaint	27
Impose a retaliatory tariff	5
Threaten	4
Threaten strongly	4
Attempt to form a cartel	1
Ban imports	1
Boycott	1
COOPERATIVE ACTIONS	
Agree partially	15
Make conciliatory statements or actions	7
Agree to negotiations	5
Agree completely	3
State that some progress has been made	3
Agree to discuss or study the issue	3
Stop some of the disputed policies	2
Agree to mediation	2
Stop all the disputed policies	2
Attempt to interest others in negotiations	1

REGIMES

Table A2-6. Regime Combinations in Trade Disputes and Non-Disputes

Combination	Frequency Disputes/Non-Disputes	
All sides adhere to the post World War II liberal trade regime	11	15
All sides adhere to the Soviet Socialist trade regime	1	0
All sides adhere to the mercantilist trade regime	2	0
All sides adhere to the South preferential trade regime	0	0
Post World War II liberal and Soviet Socialist trade regimes	1	0
Post World War II liberal and mercantilist trade regimes	8	1
Post World War II liberal and South preferential trade regimes	4	1
Post World War II liberal, Soviet socialist, and mercantilist trade regimes	0	0
Post World War II liberal, Soviet socialist, and South preferential trade regimes	0	4
Post World War II liberal, mercantilist, and South preferential trade regimes	0	5
Soviet socialist and mercantilist trade regimes	2	0
Soviet socialist and South preferential trade regimes	0	0
Soviet socialist, mercantilist, and South preferential trade regimes	0	1
Mercantilist and South preferential trade regimes	1	0
All four trade regimes	5	0

Table A2-7. Adherence to Regimes by Side

| | FREQUENCIES | | | |
| | Side's regime was coded as ... | | | |
Adherence	Post World War II Liberal	Soviet Socialist	Mercantilist	South Preferential
Very weak	13	0	8	3
Moderate	39	4	11	9
Strong	34	11	14	10

Table A2-8. Principles

PRINCIPLES BY REGIME	FREQUENCY
POST WORLD WAR II LIBERAL	
Efficiency	44
Sovereignty	41
SOVIET SOCIALIST	
Anti-imperialism	13
Soviet hegemony	3
MERCANTILIST	
Market stability	7
Hierarchy	25
SOUTH PREFERENTIAL	
Price stability	11
Equity	12

Table A2-9. Norms

NORMS BY REGIME	FREQUENCY
POST WORLD WAR II LIBERAL	
Most favored nation status	22
General system of preferences	8
Reciprocity	23
Safeguards	32
SOVIET SOCIALIST	
State trading	13
Guaranteed supplies to the Soviets	3
MERCANTILIST	
Protection of trade rights, market shares	26
MERCANTILIST AND SOUTH PREFERENTIAL	
Market regulation	19
SOUTH PREFERENTIAL	
Redistribution of resources	10

Table A2-10. Rules

RULES	FREQUENCY
UNIQUE RULES	
Post World War II Liberal Trade regime	
National treatment	3
Reciprocity	11
Balance of payments corrections	10
Uniform valuation	2
Discrimination for national security only	2
Limits on import licensing	2
Limits on technical standards	12
Limits on state trading	1
Soviet Socialist Trade Regime	
Controls on monopolies	2
Controls on capitalist states	5
State ownership	0
State monopoly on trading	6
Mercantilist Trade Regime	
Discrimination	3
South Preferential Trade Regime	
Import quotas	3
Buffer stocks	1
OVERLAPPING RULES	
Post World War II Liberal and Soviet Socialist Trade Regimes	
Limits on export licensing	1
No subsidies	9
No quotas	6
Post World War II Liberal and Mercantilist Trade Regimes	
Protection of certain sectors	33
Soviet Socialist and Mercantilist Trade Regimes	
Long-term purchase arrangements	1
Mercantilist and South Preferential Trade Regimes	
Export quotas	2
Post World War II Liberal, Soviet Socialist, and South Preferential Trade Regimes	
Special rights for LDCs	19
Non-discrimination	10
Minimum prices	3
All Four Trade Regimes	
No dumping	1
No specific rule claim made or claim was unclear	8

RELATIVE POWER

Table A2-11. Power Measures

KIND OF POWER	FREQUENCIES
ECONOMIC	
The main plaintiffs (side 1) are stronger	11
The main defendants (side 2) are stronger	29
The other participants (side 3) are stronger	0
The other participants (side 4) are stronger	0
At least 2 sides are equally strong	22
POLITICAL	
The main plaintiffs (side 1) are stronger	10
The main defendants (side 2) are stronger	39
The other participants (side 3) are stronger	2
The other participants (side 4) are stronger	1
At least 2 sides are equally strong	10

OTHER INDEPENDENT VARIABLES

Table A2-12. Other Independent variables

VARIABLES	FREQUENCIES
FRIENDLINESS OF GENERAL RELATIONS	
Unfriendly	5
Neutral or mixed	21
Friendly	36
TIME FRAME OF THE DISPUTE	
Between 1978 and 1983	14
Before 1978 to before 1983	5
Before 1978 to after 1983	17
After 1978 to after 1983	9

CONFLICT MANAGEMENT

Table A2-13. Management Variables

VARIABLES	FREQUENCIES
MANAGERS	
GATT	16
FAO	5
UNCTAD	10
International Sugar Organization	2
MEDIATION	
Unsuccessful	8
Moderately successful	10
Successful	3
Not used	24
NEGOTIATIONS	
Unsuccessful	13
Moderately successful	17
Successful	7
Not used	8

OUTCOME

Table A2-14. Outcome Variables

VARIABLES	FREQUENCIES
WINNER	
Primary defendant (side 1)	9
Primary plaintiff (side 2)	4
More than one side, but not all sides	1
No side lost	5
On-going	26
OVERALL SATISFACTION	
Mixed satisfaction and dissatisfaction among the sides	39
All sides satisfied	6

Appendix 3

Multidimensional Scaling Results and A Methodological Note on MDS

RESULTS OF MDS FROM CHAPTER 6

In Chapter 6 I presented idealized representaitons of the actual MDS results that mapped cases according to their similarity to each other. Here are the actual figures.

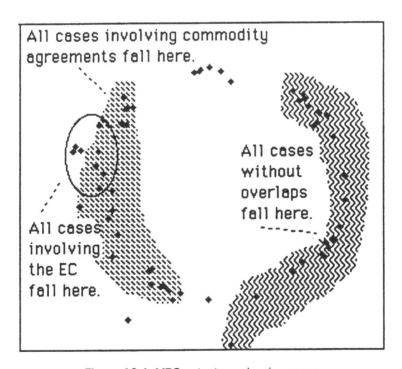

All cases involving commodity agreements fall here.

All cases without overlaps fall here.

All cases involving the EC fall here.

Figure A3-1. MDS output: overlapping cases.

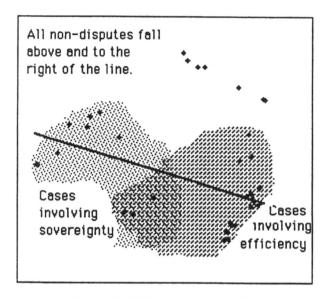

Figure A3-2. MDS output: principles.

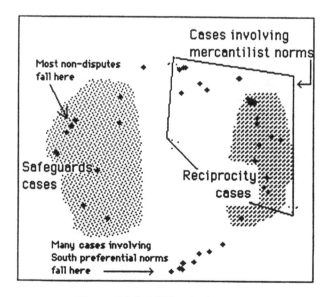

Figure A3-3. MDS output: norms.

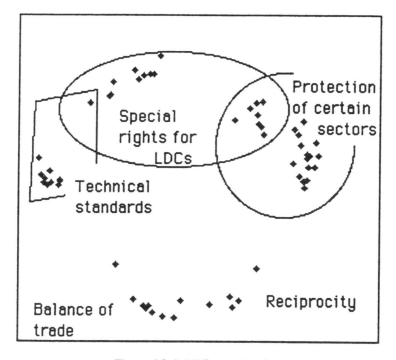

Figure A3-4. MDS output: rules.

METHODOLOGICAL NOTE ON MDS

To show how cases of food and feed trade problems are similar or distinct from each other, I use a technique called Multi-Dimensional Scaling (MDS). (See Kruskal and Wish, 1978; Schiffman, et al., 1981; Davison, 1983.) I have used the output of MDS routines as a way of describing and summarizing the differences and similarities between cases. This procedure is a form of "confirmatory" hypothesis testing (Davison, 1983:198-200).

Explanation

The classic example of how Multi-Dimensional Scaling (MDS) works involves the distances between cities "as the airplane flies." If you have three cities, and you know the distances between each pair of them, you can do a fair job of mapping where they are relative to each other. In other words, if you know the lengths of the three sides of a triangle, you can draw only one triangle. What you do not know

is where City A is relative to the directions of the compass. If . . .
  City A is 400 miles from City B,
  City A is 700 miles from City C, and
  City B is 640 miles from City C,
then the triangle linking the three cities will look like the following.

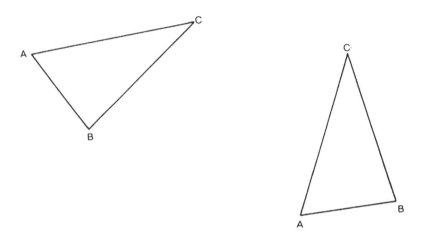

Figure A3-5. Locations of three cities.

City A may be in the north, south, east, or west. That we do not
know. We do know where Cities A, B, and C are relative to each
other.

Now extend this approach to more than three cities. A computer
algorithm (ALSCAL in SPSS) maps cities based on how close they
are to each other. Because this is a much more difficult process when
you have more than three cities, the computer searches iteratively for
the best map according to certain criteria.

The notion of distance works fine for cities, but how does it apply
to the similarities or dissimilarities of trade problems and trade
disputes? The technique was slightly different for looking at similarities based on how the issues, participants, and commodities of
cases overlapped than for looking at similarities of principles, norms,
and rules. Here is my approach for the first analysis. First I looked at
Case A and how it was coded in the data file. Specifically, I looked
at the variables that contained the names of up to five cases that
were similar to Case A. Then I looked at the same variables for Case

G. I calculated the similarity between cases as shown in the example below:

Case A overlaps with Case B.

Case G overlaps with Cases B, C, D, E, and F.

Cases A, B, C, D, E, F, and G—seven cases—are considered.

One case (B) is referenced in both cases.

The similarity score is one-seventh (one case of seven).

The process was almost the same for quantifying the similarity between cases, based on principles, norms, or rules. In comparing two cases, I looked at which principles are cited by the sides. The more principles that the two cases had in common, the more similar—the closer—the two cases were. I divide the number of principles that two cases have in common by the total number of principles referenced in the two cases. This proportion of principles in common is my measure of similarity.

Here is an example:

In Case A, principles 1, 2, 3, and 4 are referred to.

In Case G, principles 3 and 4 are referred to.

(Case G has two sides; Case A has four.)

The total number of principles in common is 2 (principles 3 and 4).

The total number of principles (1, 2, 3, and 4) is 4.

The similarity between the two cases receives a score of one-half. If, instead, Case G had involved principles 5 and 7, then the similarity score would have been 0. If Case G had involved principles 3 and 7, the similarity score would have been one-fifth. The similarity score would equal 1 only if the only principles referred to in Case A were the same as those in Case G, and vice versa. In this example, Case A might involve principles 1, 2, 1, and 1 (three of four sides referred to principle 1), while Case B involves principles 1 and 2. I followed the same procedure for calculating the similarity of cases based on norms and rules.

Analysis

MDS has two measures of goodness-of-fit, Kruskal's Stress 1 and an R^2-like statistic. However, since I am using MDS for confirmatory data analysis, the requirements for these statistics are relaxed. Of the possible algorithms for mapping the cases based on their similarity scores, I chose Euclidean models in two dimensions because I have no theoretical reason to expect a solution of more than two dimensions.

References

ARTICLES AND BOOKS

Aggarwal, V. 1983. "The Unraveling of the Multi-Fiber Arrangement, 1981: An Examination of International Regime Change." *International Organization* 37: 617–45.

——. 1985. *Liberal Protectionism: The International Politics of Organized Textile Trade.* Berkeley: University of California Press.

——, R. Keohane, and D. Yoffie. 1987. "The Dynamics of Negotiated Protectionism." *American Political Science Review* 81: 345–66.

Albert, B. and A. Graves. 1988. *The World Sugar Economy in War and Depression, 1914–1940.* New York: Routledge.

Alexander, G. 1986. "The Calypso Blues: Why the Caribbean Basin Initiative Isn't Working." *Policy Review* 38: 55–9.

Alker, H., Jr. 1981. "Dialectical Foundations of Global Disparities." *International Studies Quarterly* 25: 69–98.

——, and F. L. Sherman. 1982. "Collective Security-Seeking Practices Since 1945." *Managing International Crisis,* ed. D. Frei. Beverly Hills, CA: Sage Publishing.

Apter, D., ed. 1964. *Ideology and Discontent.* New York: The Free Press.

Azar, E. 1972. "Conflict Escalation and Conflict Reduction in an International Crisis: Suez, 1956." *Journal of Conflict Resolution* 16: 183–201.

——. 1980. "The Conflict and Peace Data Bank (COPDAB) Project." *Journal of Conflict Resolution* 24: 143–52.

Bachrach, P. and M. Baratz. 1970. *Power and Poverty: Theory and Practice.* New York: Oxford University Press.

Bloomfield, L. and A. Leiss. 1969. *Controlling Small Wars.* New York: Alfred Knopf.

Brandt Commission. 1980. *North–South: A Program for Survival.* Cambridge: MIT Press.

——. 1983. *Common Crisis North–South: Cooperation for World Recovery.* Cambridge: MIT Press.

Bueno De Mesquita, B. 1981. *The War Trap.* New Haven, CT: Yale University Press.

Burton, J. 1984. *Global Conflict: The Domestic Sources of International Crisis.* Brighton, Sussex, Great Britain: Wheatsheaf Books.

Butterworth, R. and M. Scranton. 1976. *Managing Interstate Crises, 1945–1974: Data with Synopses.* Pittsburgh: University Center for International Studies, University of Pittsburgh.

Comisso, E. 1986. "State Structures, Political Processes, and Collective Choice in CMEA States: Introduction." *International Organization* 40: 195-238.

——, and L. Tyson. 1986. *Power, Purpose, and Collective Choice: Economic Strategy in Socialist States.* Special issue of *International Organization* 40.

Conybeare, J. 1985. "A Comparative Study of Anglo-Hanse, Franco-Italian, and Hawley-Smoot Conflicts." *World Politics* 38: 147–72.

Coote, B. 1987. *The Hunger Crop: Poverty and the Sugar Industry*. Oxford: Oxfam.

Coser, L. 1956. *The Functions of Social Conflict*. London: Routledge and Kegan Paul.

Cowhey, P. 1990. "The International Telecommunications Regime: The Political Roots of High Technology." *International Organization* 44: 169–99.

Cutler, M. 1983. "East-South Relations at UNCTAD: Global Political Economy and the CMEA." *International Organization* 37: 121–42.

Dahl, R. 1976. *Modern Political Analysis*. Englewood Cliffs: Prentice-Hall.

Davison, M. 1983. *Multidimensional Scaling*. New York: John Wiley and Sons.

Dillon, S. 1984. "Sugar and Price—Editorial." *Food Policy* 9: 3.

DiLorenzo, T., V. Sementilli, and L. Southwick, Jr. 1983. "The Lomé Sugar Protocal: Increased Dependency for Fiji and the Other ACP States." *Review of Social Economy* 41: 25–38.

Dunn, J. Jr. 1987. "Automobiles in International Trade: Regime Change Or Persistence?" *International Organization* 41: 225–52.

Farris, P., H. Alker, Jr., K. Carley, and F. Sherman. 1980. *Phase/Actor Disaggregated Butterworth-Scranton Codebook*. Working paper. Cambridge: Massachusetts Institute of Technology Center for International Studies.

Finlayson, J. and M. Zacher. 1981. "The GATT and the Regulation of Trade Barriers: Regime Dynamics and Functions." *International Organization* 35: 561–602.

——, and M. Zacher. 1988. *Managing International Markets: Developing Countries and the Commodity Trade Regime*. New York: Columbia University Press.

Gilpin, R. 1975. *U.S. Power and the Multinational Corporation: The Political Economy of Foreign Direct Investment*. New York: Basic Books.

——. 1987. *The Political Economy of International Relations*. Princeton: Princeton University Press.

Haas, E. 1980. "Why Collaborate? Issue-Linkage and International Regimes." *World Politics* 32: 357–405.

——. 1983. "Regime Decay: Conflict Management and International Organizations, 1945–81." *International Organization* 35: 561–602.

Haas, P. 1989. "Do Regimes Matter? Epistemic Communities and Mediterranean Pollution Control." *International Organization* 43: 377–403.

Haggard, S. and B. Simmons. 1987. "Theories of International Regimes." *International Organization* 41: 491–517.

Holzner, B. and J. Marx. 1979. *Knowledge Application: The Knowledge System in Society*. Boston: Allyn and Bacon.

Jervis, R. 1982. "Security Regimes." *International Organization* 36: 357–78.

Johnson, H. 1968. "Ideology and the Social System." *International Encyclopedia of the Social Sciences*, ed. D. Sills, Volume 7. New York: Macmillan Company and the Free Press.

Katzenstein, P. 1984. *Corporatism and Change: Austria, Switzerland, and the Politics of Industry*. Ithaca: Cornell University Press.

Keeley, J. 1990. "Toward a Foucauldian Analysis of International Regimes." *International Organization* 44: 83–105.

Kegley, C. and G. Raymond. 1990. *When Trust Breaks Down: Alliance Norms and World Politics*. Columbia: University of South Carolina Press.

Keohane, R. 1984. *After Hegemony: Cooperation and Discord in the World Political Economy*. Princeton: Princeton University Press.

——, and J. Nye. 1977. *Power and Interdependence*. Boston: Little and Brown.

Kindleberger, C. 1986. *The World in Depression, 1929–1939*. Berkeley: University of California Press.

Krasner, S. 1982. "Structural Causes and Regimes as Intervening Variables." *International Organization* 36: 185–206.

——. 1985. *Structural Conflict: The Third World Against Global Liberalism*. Berkeley: University of California Press.

Kratochwil, F. and J. Ruggie. 1986. "International Organization: A State of the Art on an Art of the State." *International Organization* 40: 753–75.

Kruskal, J. and M. Wish. 1978. *Multidimensional Scaling*. Quantitative Applications in the Social Sciences, Volume 11. Beverly Hills, CA: Sage Publications.

Lake, D. 1988. *Power, Protection, and Free Trade: International Sources of U.S. Commercial Strategy, 1887–1939*. Ithaca: Cornell University Press.

Laszlo, E., R. Baker, Jr., E. Eisenberg, and V. Raman. 1978. *The Objectives of the New International Economic Order*. New York: Pergamon Press for UNITAR.

Lavigne, M. 1983. "The Soviet Union Inside COMECON." *Soviet Studies* 35: 135–53.

Lenin, V. 1939. *Imperialism: The Highest Stage of Capitalism*. New York: International Publishers.

Lindert, P. and C. Kindleberger. 1982. *International Economics*, 7th edition. Homewood: R.D. Irwin.

Lipson, C. 1982. "The Transformation of Trade: The Sources and Effects of Regime Change." *International Organization* 36: 417–55.

Lowi, T. 1979. *The End of Liberalism: The Second Republic of the United States*. 2nd ed. New York: W.W. Norton and Company.

Lukes, S. 1974. *Power: A Radical View*. London: The MacMillan Press.

Mahler, V. 1981. "Britain, the EC, and the Developing Commonwealth: Dependence, Interdependence and the Political-Economy of Sugar." *International Organization* 33: 467–92.

Mannheim, K. 1936. *Ideology and Utopia: An Introduction to the Sociology of Knowledge*. Translated by L. Wirth and E. Shils. New York: Harcourt, Brace.

Marlin-Bennett, R., A. Rosenblatt, and J. Wang. 1992. "The Visible Hand: The US, Japan, and the Management of Trade Disputes." *International Interactions* 17: 191–213.

Marrese, M. 1986. "CMEA: Effective but Cumbersome Political Economy." *International Organization* 40: 287–327.

Matusek, I. 1981. "Eastern Europe: Political Context." *East European Economic Assessment; Part 2—Regional Assessments: A Compendium of Papers*. US Congress Joint Economic Committee Print. 10 July. 97th Congress, 1st Session. Washington, DC: US Government Printing Office, pp. 96–106.

McClelland, C. and G. Hoggard. 1969. "Conflict Patterns in the Interactions Among Nations." *International Politics and Foreign Policy: A Reader in Research and Theory*, revised, ed. J. Rosenau. New York: The Free Press.

Mintz, S. 1985. *Sweetness and Power: The Place of Sugar in Modern History*. New York: Viking Press.

Murphy, C. 1984. *The Emergence of the NIEO Ideology*. Boulder: Westview Press.

Nicholson, M. 1967. "Tariff Wars and a Model of Conflict." *Journal of Peace Research* 1: 26–38.

Odell, J. 1985. "The Outcomes of International Trade Conflicts: The US and South Korea, 1960–1981." *International Studies Quarterly* 29: 263–86.

Olson, M. 1971. *The Logic of Collective Action*. Cambridge: Harvard University Press.

——. 1982. *The Rise and Decline of Nations: Economic Growth, Stagflation, and Social Rigidities*. New Haven: Yale University Press.

Onuf, N. 1989. *World of Our Making: Rules and Rule in Social Theory and International Relations*. Columbia: University of South Carolina Press.

Puchala, D. and R. Hopkins. 1982. "International Regimes: Lessons from Inductive Analysis." *International Organization* 36: 245–76.

Ramsay, A. 1987. "The Political Economy of Sugar in Thailand." *Pacific Affairs* 60: 248–70.

Rawls, J. 1971. *A Theory of Justice*. Cambridge: Harvard University Press.

Rhodes, C. 1989. "Reciprocity in Trade: The Utility of Bargaining Theory." *International Organization* 43: 273–300.

Rhodes-Jones, C. 1986. "Reciprocity and the GATT Regime: An Uneasy Relationship." Paper presented at a meeting of the International Studies Association, Anaheim, CA. Photocopy.

Rosenau, J. 1990. *Turbulence in World Politics: A Theory of Change and Continuity*. Princeton: Princeton University Press.

Rothstein, R. 1977. *The Weak in the World of the Strong: The Developing Countries in the International System*. New York: Columbia University Press.

——. 1984. "Regime-Creation by a Coalition of the Weak: Lessons from the NIEO and the Integrated Program for Commodities." *International Studies Quarterly* 23: 307–28.

Ruggie, J. 1982. "International Regimes, Transactions, and Change: Embedded Liberalism in the Postwar Economic Order." *International Organization* 36: 379–415.

Russett, Bruce. 1985. "The Mysterious Case of Vanishing Hegemony: or, Is Mark Twain Really Dead?" *International Organization* 39: 207–31.

Schiffman, S., L. Reynolds, and F. Young. 1981. *Introduction to Multidimensional Scaling: Theory, Methods, and Applications*. Orlando, FL: Academic Press, Inc.

Schmitter, P. 1979. "Still the Century of Corporatism?" *Trends Toward Corporatist Intermediation*, eds. P. Schmitter and G. Lehmbruch. Beverly Hills: Sage Publications.

Schuh, G. 1986. "Making Food Policy in a New International Environment." *Food Policy: Frameworks for Analysis and Action*, eds. C. Mann and B. Huddleston. Indiana: Indiana University Press.

Seabold, W. and N. Onuf. 1981. "Late Capitalism, Uneven Development, and Foreign Policy Postures." *The Political Economy of Foreign Policy Behavior*, eds. C. Kegley, Jr. and P. McGowan. Sage International Yearbook of Foreign Policy Studies, Volume 6. Beverly Hills: Sage Publications.

Sherman, F. 1987. "Part-Way to Peace: The United Nations and the Road to Nowhere?" Diss. Pennsylvania State University.

Shils, E. 1968. "The Concept and Function of Ideology." *International Encyclopedia of the Social Sciences*, ed. D. Sills, Volume 7. New York: Macmillan Company and the Free Press.

Shue, H. 1986. "Articulating 'Is' and 'Ought' for Prudent Foreign Policy Development: Regime and Responsibility." Paper presented at a meeting of the International Studies Association, Anaheim, CA. Photocopy.

Simon, H. 1976. *Administrative Behavior: A Study of Decision-Making Processes in Administrative Organization*, 3rd ed. New York: Free Press.

Singer, J. and M. Small. 1972. *The Wages of War, 1816-1965: A Statistical Handbook*. New York: Wiley.

Smith, I. 1981. "EEC Sugar Policy in an International Context." *Journal of World Trade Law* 15: 95-110.

——. 1983. "Prospects for a New International Sugar Agreement." *Journal of World Trade Law* 17: 308-24.

Smith, R. 1987. "Explaining the Non-Proliferation Regime: Anomalies for Contemporary International Relations Theory." *International Organization* 41: 253-81.

Snyder, G. and P. Diesing. 1977. *Conflict Among Nations: Bargaining, Decision Making, and System Structure in International Crises*. Princeton: Princeton University Press.

Staber, U. 1987. "Corporatism and the Governance Structure of American Trade Associations." *Political Studies* 35: 278-88.

Strange, S. 1982. "Cave! Hic Dragones: A Critique of Regime Analysis." *International Organization* 36: 479-96.

——. 1985. "Protectionism and World Politics." *International Organization* 39: 233-59.

——. 1987. "The Persistent Myth of Lost Hegemony." *International Organization* 41: 551-74.

Talbot, R. 1978. *The Chicken War: An International Trade Conflict Between the United States and the European Community, 1961-64*. Ames: Iowa State University Press.

Tetreault, M. 1988. "Regimes and Liberal World Orders." *Alternatives* 13: 5-26.

Thompson, J. 1967. *Organizations in Action*. New York: McGraw-Hill.

Tomich, D. 1990. *Slavery in the Circuit of Sugar: Martinique and the World Economy, 1830-1848*. Baltimore: Johns Hopkins University Press.

Tsadik, T. 1982. "The International Sugar Market: Self-Sufficiency or Free Trade?" *Journal of World Trade Law* 16: 133-51.

United States Cuban Sugar Council. 1948. *Sugar: Facts and Figures*. New York: United States Cuban Sugar Council.

Valdés, A. and J. Zietz. 1980. *Agricultural Protection in OECD Countries: Its Cost to Less-Developed Countries*. Research Report 21. Washington, DC: International Food Policy Research Institute.

Walker, R. 1984. *Culture, Ideology, and World Order*. Boulder: Westview Press.

Young, O. 1980. "International Regimes: Problems of Concept Formation." *World Politics* 32: 331–56.

———. 1982. *Resource Regimes: Natural Resources and Social Institutions*. Berkeley: University of California Press.

Zacher, M. 1987. "Trade Gaps, Analytical Gaps: Regime Analysis and International Commodity Trade Regulation." *International Organization* 41: 173–202.

Zietz, J. and A. Valdés. 1986. *The Costs of Protectionism to Developing Countries: An Analysis for Selected Agricultural Products*. Washington, D.C.: World Bank.

EUROPEAN COMMUNITY DOCUMENTS AND PUBLICATIONS

Commission of the European Communities. "Lomé Convention of 28 February 1975." *The Courier* 31 (1975). Special issue with full text of the convention.

———. Directorate-General for Information. *Sugar, the European Community, and the Lomé Convention*. February 1983, X/64/83.

———. Secretariat. *Bulletin of the European Communities*. Various issues, 1978–1983.

———. Secretariat. *Green Europe: Newsletter of the Common Agricultural Policy*. Various numbers, 1978–1983.

———. Secretariat. Statistical Office. *Analytical Tables of Foreign Trade, NIMEXE*. Various issues.

European Parliament. "Report Drawn up on Behalf of the Committee on External Economic Relations on the Impact of the CAP on the External Relations of the European Community." In *Working Documents*, 1983–1984, 10 May 1983, 1–248/83/B.

GENERAL AGREEMENT ON TARIFFS AND TRADE DOCUMENTS AND PUBLICATIONS

Contracting Parties to the General Agreement on Tariffs and Trade. *Activities of the GATT*. Various issues, 1978–1984.

———. "Arrangement Regarding International Trade in Textiles." *Basic Instruments and Selected Documents*, 21st Supplement. Decisions, Reports, 1973–1974, and 30th Session. Geneva: Contracting Parties to the General Agreement on Tariffs and Trade, February 1975. Cited, with the Protocols extending this Arrangement, as the Multi-Fiber Arrangement or MFA.

———. "Generalized System of Preferences." *Basic Instruments and Selected Documents*, 18th Supplement. Protocols, Decisions, Reports, 1970–1971, and 27th Session. Geneva: Contracting Parties to the General Agreement on Tariffs and Trade, April 1972.

———. "Protocol Extending the Arrangement Regarding International Trade in Textiles." *Basic Instruments and Selected Documents*, 24th Supplement.

Protocols, Decisions, Reports, 1976–1977, and 33rd Session. Geneva: Contracting Parties to the General Agreement on Tariffs and Trade, January 1978.

—— . "Protocol Extending the Arrangement Regarding International Trade in Textiles." *Basic Instruments and Selected Documents,* 28th Supplement. Protocols, Decisions, Reports, 1980–1981, and 37th Session. Geneva: Contracting Parties to the General Agreement on Tariffs and Trade, March 1982.

—— . "Text of the General Agreement in Force in 1969." *Basic Instruments and Selected Documents,* Volume 4. Geneva: Contracting Parties to the General Agreement on Tariffs and Trade, 1969.

—— . [Tokyo Round Agreements]. *Basic Instruments and Selected Documents,* 26th Supplement. Protocols, Decisions, and Reports, 1978–1979, and 35th Session. Geneva: Contracting Parties to the General Agreement on Tariffs and Trade, March 1980. Includes the following:

"Agreement on Government Procurement;"
"Agreement on Implementation of Article VII;"
"Agreement on Import Licensing Procedures;"
"Agreement on Interpretation and Application of Articles VI, XVI, and XXIII [Subsidies Code];"
"Agreement on Technical Barriers to Trade;"
"Arrangement Regarding Bovine Meat;"
"Declaration on Trade Measures Taken for Balance of Payments Purposes;"
"International Dairy Arrangement."

SOVIET DOCUMENT AND PUBLICATION

Union of Soviet Socialist Republics. "Constitution (Fundamental Law) of the Union of Soviet Socialist Republics." Adopted at the 7th (Special) Session of the Supreme Soviet of the USSR, 9th Convocation, 7 October 1977. Moscow: Novosti Press Agency, 1977.

—— . Ministry of Foreign Trade. *Foreign Trade.* Various issues, 1978–1983.

UNITED NATIONS DOCUMENTS AND PUBLICATIONS

United Nations. Conference on Trade and Development. "Annex VII: Documents Submitted to the Conference by Certain Groups of Countries." *1979 Proceedings.* Cited as "Document."

—— . Conference on Trade and Development. *International Sugar Agreement of 1984,* TD/SUGAR.10/11/rev/1 1985.

—— . Conference on Trade and Development. Trade and Development Board. *Official Records,* 17th through 27th Sessions, 1978–1983.

—— . Conference on Trade and Development. Trade and Development Board. "Protectionism and Structural Adjustment in the Agricultural Sectors: Progress Report by the UNCTAD Secretariat." *Official Records,*

24th Session, 8–24 March 1982, 11–18 May 1982, and 30 June-2 July 1982, Annexes, 18 February 1982, TD/B/885.

———. Conference on Trade and Development. Trade and Development Board. "Report of the Ad Hoc Intergovernmental Committee for the Integrated Programme for Commodities." *Official Records*, 22nd Session, 9–20 March 1981, Annexes, 27 October 1980, TD/B/IPC/AC/35.

———. Conference on Trade and Development. Trade and Development Board. "Report of the Committee on Commodities on Its First Special Session." *Official Records*, 25th Session, Supplement no. 2, 8–12 February 1983, TD/B/894.

———. Conference on Trade and Development. "Report of the Committee on Commodities on Its Tenth Session." *Official Records*, 26th Session, Supplement no. 4, 26 January–8 February 1983, TD/B/944; TD/B/C.1/247.

———. Department of International Economic and Social Affairs. Statistical Office. *International Trade Statistics Yearbook*. Various issues.

———. Department of International Economic and Social Affairs. Statistical Office. *Statistical Yearbook*, 1982.

———. Food and Agriculture Organization. *FAO Trade Yearbook*, 1978–1984.

———. Food and Agriculture Organization. *The State of Food and Agriculture*. Various issues, 1978–1983.

UNITED STATES DOCUMENTS AND PUBLICATION

United States. Department of Agriculture. *Foreign Agriculture*. Various issues, 1978–1983.

———. Department of Agriculture. Economic Research Service. Agricultural Trade and Analysis Division. USSR Section. *Database on Soviet Trade*. Project led by K. Zeimetz.

———. General Accounting Office. *Sugar and Other Sweeteners: An Industry Assessment*. Washington: U.S. General Accounting Office, 1979.

WORLD BANK PUBLICATION

World Bank. *World Development Report*, 1988. Oxford: Oxford University Press.

Index

*For Product Safety Concerns and Information please contact
our EU representative GPSR@taylorandfrancis.com Taylor & Francis
Verlag GmbH, Kaufingerstraße 24, 80331 München, Germany*

T - #0022 - 270225 - C0 - 234/156/11 [13] - CB - 9780415567138 - Gloss Lamination